Y0-BDP-306

JUL 23 2015 ✓

PUBLIC LIBRARY

EXPLORING
OLD HIGHWAY No. 1 WEST

Canada's Route 66

CREDITS

EDITOR: Doug Whiteway
EDITORIAL ASSISTANCE: Peter St. John
PROJECT MANAGEMENT: Barbara Huck
DESIGN AND LAYOUT: Bergdís Sigurðardóttir
MAPS: Dawn Huck
PREPRESS AND PRINTING: Friesens Corporation, Canada
FRONT COVER PHOTOGRAPHS: Peter St. John and Canstockphoto
BACK COVER PHOTOGRAPH: Jenny Baker

LIBRARY AND ARCHIVES CANADA CATALOGUING IN PUBLICATION

Saunders, J. Clark, 1948-, author
Exploring old Highway No. 1 West : Canada's Route 66 : your guide to scenic trips
& adventures along the original Trans-Canada Highway / J. Clark Saunders.
Includes bibliographical references.
ISBN 978-1-896150-76-5 (pbk.)

1. Trans-Canada Highway – Guidebooks.
2. Trans-Canada Highway – History.
3. Automobile travel – Canada, Western – Guidebooks.
4. Canada, Western – Description and travel. I. Title.

FC76.S28 2014   917.1204'4   C2014-901292-6

Heartland Associates would like to thank Manitoba Culture, Heritage
and Tourism for its continued assistance and support.

Heartland Associates, Inc.
PO Box 103, RPO Corydon
Winnipeg, Manitoba, Canada R3M 3S3
www.heartlandbooks.ca
hrtland@mts.net

FSC
www.fsc.org
MIX
Paper from
responsible sources
FSC® C016245

ENVIRONMENTAL BENEFITS STATEMENT

Heartland Associates Inc saved the following
resources by printing the pages of this book on
chlorine free paper made with 10% post-consumer
waste.

TREES	WATER	ENERGY	SOLID WASTE	GREENHOUSE GASES
2	781	1	53	144
FULLY GROWN	GALLONS	MILLION BTUs	POUNDS	POUNDS

Environmental impact estimates were made using the Environmental Paper Network
Paper Calculator 3.2. For more information visit www.papercalculator.org.

J. CLARK SAUNDERS

EXPLORING

OLD HIGHWAY No. 1 WEST

Canada's Route 66

YOUR GUIDE TO SCENIC TRIPS & ADVENTURES
ALONG THE ORIGINAL TRANS-CANADA HIGHWAY

Heartland

Winnipeg, Manitoba

Printed in Manitoba, Canada

A typical mid-1950s family car.

Ryan Sardachuk / Fastlane Illustration

Stan Milosovic Collection

Portage Avenue, in downtown Winnipeg, at the beginning of the nifty 1950s.

To my brothers, Tom and Allan, the travelling companions of my childhood, and to those of my riper years, Warren McDougall and Doug Whiteway.

CONTENTS

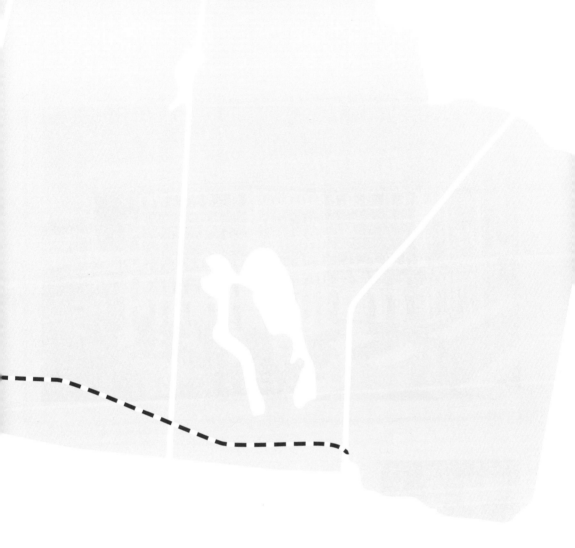

4:—"THE ROYAL ALEXANDRA" CANADIAN PACIFIC RAILWAY'S HOTEL. WINNIPEG. MANITOBA.

40478

Stan Milosovic / Vintage Images of Manitoba

NORTH SHORE MARINE DRIVE AT FISHERMAN'S COVE. VANCOUVER. B. C., CANADA

West Vancouver Archives / Marine Drive at Fisherman's Cove, 1948 / 3610.wva.pho

PREFACE

To locate the genesis of this book I would have to go back to the days of my earliest childhood memories in the early 1950s. As a baby boomer living most of those years in Winnipeg, Manitoba, and with both sets of grandparents living in Victoria, British Columbia (not to mention a slew of other relatives on the West Coast), I had occasion to travel Old No. 1 West, the precursor of the Trans-Canada Highway, across Western Canada with my family more than once. Between 1956 and 1960, when my parents, older and younger brothers and I lived in West Vancouver, we travelled in the other direction to see friends in Winnipeg. By the late 1960s, the end of the period covered in this book, we were living in Winnipeg again, but our road trips across the western half of the country continued.

Among the more recent experiences that spurred me to action on this book was a journey undertaken with friends a few years ago to explore Route 66 in the United States. America's "Mother Road" — from Chicago in the Midwest to Santa Monica on the shores of the Pacific—has been the subject of numerous books. Among these are guidebooks that draw the attention of travellers to things to watch for along the way and help them to make sense of what they see. By contrast, the origins of the Trans-Canada Highway (though not ignored by writers, as the list of sources at the end of this volume attests) has not so far inspired a book of this kind.

Often, as I have gone in search of the TCH as it was between 1945 and 1965, I have been prompted to recall places my family encountered and experiences we shared with many other families who hit the open road when the postwar world finally allowed them to do so. My search led me not only to sections of road that have been superseded by sleeker, grander highways, but also to businesses that catered to travellers a half-century or more ago and are still there. The world around these motels, restaurants and attractions has changed vastly (and in many cases they themselves have undergone a significant transformation), but a surprising number of reminders of those early days of highway travel have survived.

In undertaking this project, I decided to limit myself to the half of the country that left me with personal memories from the days of my childhood when I travelled across it with my family. Perhaps someone, recalling the Trans-Canada Highway east from the Manitoba-Ontario boundary to St. John's, Newfoundland, as it was in those far-off days, will pick up the challenge of preparing a complementary volume.

Opposite: Midcentury sights along Old Highway No. 1—Winnipeg's grand Royal Alexandra Hotel (above), built in 1906 and demolished in 1971, and West Vancouver's picturesque Marine Drive (below) in 1948.

CANADA
in the POSTWAR WORLD

Above: The Red Ensign, Canada's flag until 1965.

Opposite: 1956 Dodge La Femme rear fender and tailfin.

When the Second World War came to an end in 1945 no one had yet managed to traverse the entire breadth of Canada by road. Most of the roads that existed were graded at best, not paved. Anyone who attempted to drive across Western Canada would have followed a route (where a route existed at all) that was in many places quite different from the one followed by today's Trans-Canada or No. 1 Highway. Yet 17 years later, when the Rogers Pass section through the Selkirk Mountains of B.C. was opened, it was possible to travel all the way across the four western provinces on pavement. Today's Trans-Canada Highway follows essentially the same route through Western Canada that it did in 1962 when Rogers Pass was opened to vehicular traffic.

Canada was a very different country those long years ago. Until the very end of the period covered by this book, the flag that flew over the country was the Red Ensign; it was only in 1965 that, after bitter controversy, the Maple Leaf flag was adopted as the nation's banner. In those days, when we sang "O Canada", we stood on guard four times (now it's only three) and we hadn't yet decided to ask God to keep our land glorious and free; the old version of the anthem just assumed that it was and would continue to be.

William Lyon Mackenzie King was prime minister when the period opened; Lester Pearson was at the helm when it ended; in between were Louis St. Laurent and John Diefenbaker. By the early '60s, the Quiet Revolution had begun to stir in Quebec and both peaceful and violent expressions of separatism had led to Anglo-Canadians asking (rhetorically, at least) what Quebec wanted.

Internationally, these were the days of the Cold War at its coldest. From the McCarthyism of the early 1950s to the Cuban missile crisis

Opposite: Christopher Ziemnowicz / www.en.wikipedia.org

TRAVEL
Canadian Pacific
ACROSS CANADA!

Canadian Pacific Archives

a decade later, the Red Scare manifested itself in a variety of ways. While some people built fallout shelters, the children of the many families who could not afford such luxuries were taught to "duck and cover" when the bomb fell, in the hope that this technique would save them from the consequences of a nuclear holocaust. Yet, despite the mushroom cloud in the background, most Canadians went about their daily lives with a remarkable spirit of optimism and confidence.

Of the things that bound the country together, the Canadian Pacific Railway was about 80 years old when the period began. For people who wanted to cross the country, it was the preferred mode of travel, most of the roads being rough and ready, and air travel being still something of a novelty and, for most people, prohibitively expensive.

Most Canadians listened to the radio. But beginning in 1952, the Canadian Broadcasting Corporation expanded into television broadcasting and black-and-white TV rapidly became a standard feature in most house- holds. Of course, remote controls would come later. In those days, after waiting for the set to warm up, viewers had to walk right up to it every time they wanted to change the channel—not that there were many channels to choose from. The broadcast day might not begin until late in the afternoon and usu- ally ended when decent people went to bed. When nothing was being broadcast viewers could gaze at the CBC test pattern. It featured a First Nations person (erroneously called an "Indian" at that time) in full headdress.

In the 1950s, kids would end the school day by put- ting down their "Dick and Jane" readers and heading home to watch *The Canadian Howdy Doody Show* and *Maggie Muggins*. They might also follow Amer- ican shows like *Superman, The Lone Ranger* and *Roy Rogers*. After supper, they could sit down with their parents as the family tuned in to *Father Knows Best* or *Leave It to Beaver.* On Sunday evenings, Canadians stayed home in large numbers to watch Ed Sullivan. By the 1960s, there would be an occasional Wayne and Shuster special to look forward to. And for something more serious there was the long-running quiz show, *Front Page Challenge,* hosted by the urbane and seemingly ageless Fred Davis. Davis welcomed guests who tried to stump a panel that included as regulars author Pierre Berton and a crusty journalist named Gordon Sinclair.

The children of the families who watched these shows were the baby boomers. Typically they were born to parents who married dur- ing or shortly after the Second World War. Because of the war, some

Above: Howdy Doody, puppet TV star of the 1950s.

Opposite: In 1947, Canadian Pacific Railway marketed its national service with this dramatic poster. In the West, at least, rail was by far the best way to travel.

NBC Photo / www.en.wikipedia.org

Canstockphoto/CSP - 5997140

With the dawning of the Space Age in the 1950s, the mundane family car began to sprout wings, turbines, and chrome-plated ornamentation of all kinds.

young couples had put off having children and had to make up for lost time. The school population rose in the 1950s and would continue to do so until the effects of "the pill" began to be felt in the late 1960s.

The population growth of the 1950s was manifested by a flight to the suburbs. It was a trend that saw housing developments mushroom and shopping centres sprout up. In larger cities, downtown cores began to struggle to remain competitive.

After the Canadian population adjusted to peacetime, many middle-class families came to benefit from a period of postwar prosperity. The automotive industry, having been dedicated to the production of military vehicles during the latter years of the war, retooled once again and started producing cars for these growing families to drive around in. Family holidays became the order of the day. And while some would go to a summer cottage and others would go camping in provincial and national parks, many took to the open road and drove across a province or two—or even four—to visit grandparents and aunts and uncles and cousins and friends or simply to explore the wonder and beauty of the vast land in which they lived.

In the postwar years, the family car truly came of age. As historian Robert Collins wrote in 1969 in *A Great Way to Go: The Automobile in Canada*, "Some of us were conceived in it; a few are born in it; many die in it."

With the war over, the car began affecting what Canadian families did and the way they did it. Going for a drive on a Sunday afternoon became a popular and inexpensive pastime. Taking the whole family out for a meal was something that could be accomplished without leaving the vehicle. (The first A&W restaurant in the country began providing roadside burgers at an outlet in Winnipeg in 1956, while the White Spot chain did the same thing on the West Coast in the same decade.)

Drive-in theatres affected the way some movie-lovers pursued their interest and likely contributed to the first of the three phenomena that Collins identifies (see above).

Suburban shopping centres made sense only in a society where most shoppers travelled by car. In those suburbs and in outlying areas accommodations sprang up along the roadsides, some of them calling themselves "motor hotels" or the elided "motels". Advertisers took to proclaiming their goods and services on billboards in sight of passing traffic. An entire industry sprang up to provide for the needs of an ever-expanding motoring public.

By the early 1960s, the Trans-Canada Highway was a long sinuous thread that enabled that motoring public to travel from sea to sea. In his introduction to *Silver Highway*, a book published in 1988 to mark the highway's 25th anniversary, Norm Rosen captured something of the mystique of the open road in general and of the TCH in particular when he wrote, "Over the years the Trans-Canada Highway has been the road to freedom and adventure for millions of Canadians." He went on, "it is a vibrant, beautiful creation dedicated to the freedom to travel without restriction from coast to coast. It is a shining example of the spirit of Canadian life—totally free from horizon to horizon; a concrete symbol of the Canadian lifestyle."

That lifestyle has since faced challenges that those rhapsodic words could not have anticipated over 25 years ago. In 1988, the impact of Middle Eastern oil prices, 9/11 and global warming lay in the future. The freedom that a car and a highway represented had come to be taken for granted and showed no sign of being curtailed.

THE LONG ROAD TO THE LONG ROAD

The building of the Canadian Pacific Railway in the late 19th century has been described by Pierre Berton as "the national dream". Notwithstanding political scandals and financial setbacks, it was accomplished in a remarkably short period of time.

The building of the Trans-Canada Highway was a very different story. To be sure, many of the same factors that had presented problems for the construction of the CPR—the necessity of federal-provincial cooperation, the changing policies of a variety of governments at different levels, the financial challenges, the lack of a single vision on the part of those in a position to make decisions—contributed to the protracted nature of the project. But there was the additional fact that, through the first half of the 20th century, only a handful of enthusiasts saw the construction of a transcontinental highway as a worthwhile project at all. The result was an on-again, off-again process that took decades to gather momentum. As a highway gradually took shape, it consisted, in many places, of stitching together already existing roads and bringing them up to a certain standard.

The advent of the automobile at the turn of the 20th century led to motorists feeling the need for decent roads on which to travel. Had the economy depended on road

This image of railroad financier Donald A. Smith is one of the iconic images of Canadian history. For more on this event, which took place at Craigallachie, B.C. on November 7, 1885, see page 136.

Ross, Alexander, Best & Co., Winnipeg / www.en.wikipedia.org

wheels

Clark Saunders

A**UTOMOTIVE MATERIALS AND TECHNOLOGY HAVE COME A LONG WAY.** When did your radiator last boil dry? And how long has it been since you had to top up your oil between changes? In the cars of the post-Second World War decades these were not uncommon occurrences. In those days, drivers and passengers had to travel long distances without the benefits of GPS, cruise control or air conditioning. On a hot summer's day, the windows would be rolled down (front corner windows would be angled to take advantage of the breeze) and an elbow—usually male—could be seen projecting from the driver's window. The driver's fingers might even be beating a tattoo on the roof. In an era when smoking was socially acceptable, the car ashtrays might require emptying at every stop. Kids might fight over who got to sit in the front; when it was time to switch, there was no need to stop because there were no seatbelts to impede children who wanted to climb forward or backward over the front seatback. It was a bench seat, of course—none of those bucket affairs. And if the occupants numbered more than four, it was probably Mom who got stuck balancing her feet on the hump that ran down the middle of the car floor.

The speedometer measured miles, not kilometres, and the speed limit on the highway was as likely to be 50 miles per hour (or mph) as 60. And in an age when highways went through many towns where speed had to be reduced to 35, no wonder it took so much longer to get anywhere.

Some might say that it was in the postwar era that the car came into its own in North America. Production had declined during the Depression, and in 1941, Canada's wartime government decreed an end to the manufacturing of automobiles for civilians. When the war ended my parents' experience was typical. Their first postwar car was a pre-war Dodge in a typically dark pre-war colour with an odd assortment of pre-war tires. Returning servicemen brought with them a demand for something better. The first seven years of the postwar era saw a return to automobile production that doubled the number of cars on Canadian roads. By the end of the 1950s, most households in the country owned a car and an increasing number had two.

Most of these cars would have been American makes. But my Scottish-born father, besides having a sentimental attachment to things British, was attracted by the fact that cars from Britain were exempt from import duties. His next two cars after the ancient Dodge were little Austins—not the most practical vehicle either for driving in Canadian winters or for taking a family of five on a cross-country odyssey. (A roof rack, perched precariously on the curved roof, was needed to carry excess baggage.)

By 1957, Dad gave in and bought a Ford Fairlane with a scintillating gold stripe on the side and understated tailfins.

The fins were perhaps the most striking design feature associated with the cars of the '50s, though they were actually inaugurated by Cadillac in 1948. The decade was noted for the introduction of two-toned paint schemes, wrap-around windows and an abundance of chrome, culminating in hood ornaments that spoke of the space age. With headlights like eyes and grills like mouths, the cars of the period were a gift to Disney and other animators who brought them to life in cartoons, though the appearance of double headlights in 1958 made the cartoonist's task a bit more challenging. Stylistic changes were introduced annually and car enthusiasts eagerly awaited the appearance of the new models. We would be halfway through the '60s before issues of safety, efficiency, and pollution control would begin to draw as much attention as style.

Charles01 / www.en.wikipedia.org

Morven / www.en.wikipedia.org

Above: The cars author Clark Saunders recalls from his childhood: a 1953 Austin A-30 (top) and a 1957 Ford Fairlane.

Opposite: Automobiles of the 1950s, lovingly preserved.

transport, progress might have been made more quickly, but as it was—and for the foreseeable future—rail would continue to be the preferred method for moving freight. But the motorists, who grew in numbers over the course of the century, represented first a moneyed class and then increasingly a middle class for whom the car simply offered some of the privileges of independence. No longer tied to railway timetables, people who could afford a car could come and go at will. But they could travel great distances only when the roads were in place to convey them to faraway places.

Shortly before the First World War, the good roads movement, along with various national and local automobile clubs and associations, began to advocate for more and better roads in general and for a transcontinental highway in particular. As early as 1912, arguments were being made for a highway that would have its western terminus at Alberni (or Port Alberni) on Vancouver Island. But the number of vehicles on Canadian roads at the time (fewer than 50,000 in the whole country) hardly seemed to warrant the kind of expense that would be involved. Consequently only 16 kilometres of non-urban paved road could be found in Canada that year. To draw attention to the fact that the car was here to stay—and to the importance of attending to the needs of motorists—the Canadian Highway Association offered a gold medal to the first motorists who would drive an all-Canadian route from sea to sea. The medal was donated by A. E. Todd, president of the Victoria Automobile Club.

The Todd Medal, offered in 1912 to the first motorist to drive across Canada sea to sea, wasn't awarded until 1946.

Courtesy of Mark Richardson

First to attempt to collect the Todd medal were Thomas Wilby, a middle-aged British writer, and Jack Haney, a young American mechanic recently moved to Canada. Haney worked for Ransom E. Olds (founder of the REO Motor Car Company). The company offered an REO special touring car, with Haney as driver-mechanic for the journey. Having travelled from Halifax to Victoria in the fall of 1912, Haney and Wilby were able to pour a bottle of Atlantic water into the Pacific at journey's end. But the trip was far from a resounding success. The travelling companions were not temperamentally well suited, and it became clear that Wilby was eager to claim all the credit for their achievement, while leaving all the work to Haney. And because long stretches of the journey were accomplished by resorting to such strategies as taking a steamer the length of Lake Superior, loading the vehicle onto trains (for example, from Fort William to Winnipeg) and making a short detour into the United States, Wilby and Haney did not qualify for the gold medal.

The years immediately before the First World War saw the inauguration of the Canadian Automobile Association (CAA) and the creation of the Canadian Good Roads Association. But the goals of these organizations took a back seat to a different set of priorities during wartime. It was not until 1919 that the Canada Highway Act provided $20 million of federal money to assist the provinces in the construction of roads generally. The provinces set to work building a system of trunk highways that did not necessarily line up at provincial boundaries with those being built by their neighbours.

Canstockphoto/CSP - 0256362

A 1956 Chevrolet Bel Air. The era of the two-tone car.

Chief among promoters of a national highway during the interwar years was Dr. Perry Doolittle, who headed the CAA from 1920 until his death in 1933. He himself managed to cross the country three times, but the necessity of "cheating" by taking a few detours denied him the gold medal. In 1925, Ed Flickenger was able to drive 4,000 miles in a Model T Ford, making use of flanged wheels on rail lines to get across northern Ontario and the Rockies. He, too, was not able to make the journey entirely by road. No gold medal for him.

In the 1930s, partly as an effort to stimulate the economy, Ottawa doled out another $20 million for provincial trunk highways. Of the highways constructed as Depression-era relief work in the West, none was more ambitious than the Big Bend highway along the Columbia River in British Columbia, completed in 1940.

By that time, another war had intervened to slow both automobile production and highway construction. It was not until 1946 that the Todd gold medal first offered in 1912 was finally collected by two veterans of the recent war: R. A. Macfarlane and his sidekick, Kenneth MacGillivray. Driving a Chevrolet Stylemaster supplied by the manufacturer for advertising purposes, the two managed to travel from Louisburg, Nova Scotia, to Victoria without resorting to railway tracks. Even then, it could hardly be said that the country was spanned by a Trans-Canada Highway worthy of the name.

The Dominion-Provincial Conference on Reconstruction in 1945

Canstockphoto/CSP - 11718032

The stamp issued in 1962 to mark the official opening of the Trans-Canada Highway.

was the first step toward the Trans Canada [*sic*] Highway Act that, four years later, made it clear that a concerted effort was to be made to stitch a proper transcontinental highway together. The act laid down the standards that construction was expected to meet. It was to be a hard-surfaced, all-weather road consisting of at least two lanes. It was to be 24 feet wide with 10-foot gravel shoulders, curves of not more than three degrees and grades of not more than six per cent. Ottawa was to pay 50 per cent of the estimated $300 million cost (and 100 per cent of the cost in national parks), while each province was to choose the shortest practicable route across its territory. The target date for completion was 1956. By the time that year arrived, the goal—notably in areas like Northern Ontario and Newfoundland—remained unmet. In an effort to speed up the work in places where no previous road existed, the act was amended by parliament to provide for an additional 40 per cent contribution from the federal government on 10 per cent of the mileage in each province.

In the event, Saskatchewan was the first province to meet the standard set out in 1949, and even there the goal was not achieved until 1957. By 1960, only about 60 per cent of the highway had reached the prescribed standards and the cost had risen to $586 million. Five years later—the end of the period covered by this book—the price tag had reached nearly a billion dollars, and there was still some paving to be done north of Superior.

In the meantime, government officials had gone ahead with the official opening of the highway. The finishing of the Rogers Pass section of the No. 1 Highway in British Columbia—replacing the much longer Big Bend—was generally regarded as the effective completion of Canada's national road. In fact, its formal opening in the summer of 1962 was said to mark the completion of the longest national highway in the world.

Something of the significance of postwar highway construction in Western Canada is summed up by Edwin C. Guillet in the conclusion to his 1966 book, *The Story of Canadian Roads*. "Calgarians," he wrote, "gave up their traditional holiday resorts on the lakes of Idaho and Montana, and played instead in the Okanagan Valley, only three or four hours away by the new good roads. If they wanted to carry on to the Pacific, Vancouver was only a 24-hour trip." Canadians, he added, could now travel inside their own country as they never had before. Recalling the description of the CPR as a ribbon of steel, Guillet went on to state that "Canada could start her second century with a new tie, a ribbon this time of concrete and asphalt, a unity based on road and wheel."

By the time those words were written, "Canada's Main Street" through the four Western provinces linked the cities of Winnipeg, Regina, Calgary, Vancouver and Victoria, as well as many smaller communities. But, in ways large and small, the highway often carved out a different route in the early postwar years from the one it takes today. The small changes that have been made over the years have often involved bypassing a town rather than slowing down to go through it, or smoothing out a path that formerly followed the contours of every hill or traced the section lines that marked the borders of prairie farms. More major changes can be seen in such sections as the routes between the Manitoba-Ontario boundary and Winnipeg, between Winnipeg and Portage la Prairie, between Calgary and Canmore and between Golden and Revelstoke. Where the old routes still exist, the following chapters take account of them. Where landmarks that were spotted by travellers in the two decades after the Second World War can still be seen, many are noted. A number of businesses that catered to the travelling public along the No. 1 Highway prior to 1965 are still in operation; a sampling is found in these pages.

Old No. 1 West was longer, narrower, slower and more winding than today's Trans-Canada. Getting stuck behind a slow-moving vehicle on what was almost entirely two-lane highway did not help to speed the journey. All things considered, setting out on a cross-country road trip was a more daunting prospect than it is now. But for those who came of age in those years, the journeys made memories.

W HEN THE PRAIRIE LANDSCAPE BECAME MIND-NUMBINGLY INTERMINABLE, **WHAT DID PEOPLE DO TO PASS THE TIME?** Before IPods, before CDs, before tapes, before eight-tracks, before many cars even had radios, what kept children—and their parents—from going stir crazy in the confinement of the family sedan as the miles and hours crept by?

Well, some resorted to pastimes of one kind or another. Counting telephone polls was simple and, in the absence of sheep, may have acted as a soporific. Counting the cars in a train might be slightly more challenging, especially if it was going in the opposite direction to the car. One year, my brother kept track of the provincial and state licence plates that we encountered. The parking lot at Lake Louise proved to be a goldmine.

Some children developed rituals—like lifting their feet off the floor or holding their breath (or both) while going through an underpass. But entire families could pass the time by singing songs (if they were musically inclined) or playing games. Of the former, "I've Been Working on the Railroad" and "Found a Peanut" were often trotted out for an airing. But counting-down songs like "Ten Green Bottles" could be just as boring as the scenery.

Some played games like "Twenty Questions" and "Geography". In the latter, you had to name a place that begins with the letter that ends the last player's entry. The problem is that most places that begin with "A" also end with "A." How many times can you use Appomattox and Adirondacks?

Then there were cumulative games. The version our family used was called "I Packed My Trunk for Boston." The first player had to think of something beginning with "A" while the next would have to add something beginning with "B" while including the first player's submission, thus: "I packed my trunk for Boston and in it I put a button and an aardvark." The person who got stuck with "X" not only had to remember 23 previously packed items but would be forced to draw on a small selection of familiar objects such as xylophones and X-rays.

"I Spy" was a perennial favorite. When children were too young to spell, you could spy things of a particular colour. When the young fry had become at least semi-literate, the initial letter of an item would be used. When my brother—the same one who listed his licence plate sightings—was still in the primary grades he spied something beginning with "T." We guessed trains and trucks and the aforementioned telephone polls. But nothing doing. He had us stumped. When we were obliged to give up, he announced triumphantly, "A tyurch!"

I've Been Working on the Railroad

I've Been Working on the Railroad
Geography
Ten Green Bottles
Found a Peanut
I Packed My Trunk for Boston
Twenty questions
SOLO.
Ter pass de time a - way.

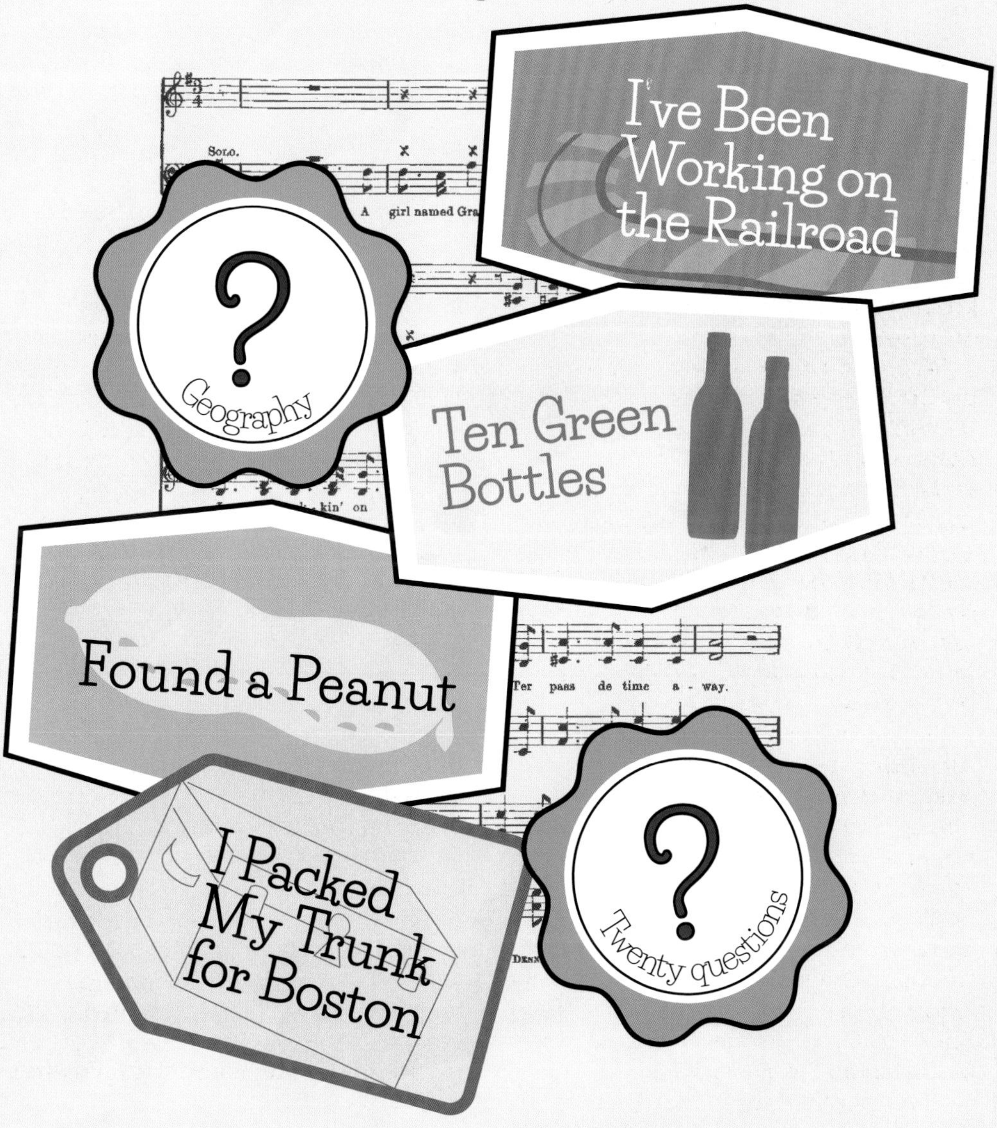

from the
ONTARIO-MANITOBA
BORDER to -
WINNIPEG

T he journey begins as it will end: with signs of humanity—some might call it civilization—intruding on a world of water, rocks and trees.

Travelling westward on the modern Trans-Canada Highway in Northwestern Ontario, motorists approaching the Manitoba boundary will be able to make out bits and pieces of broken pavement in the woods on the right. These are the remains of the old No. 1. When the Manitoba-shaped sign welcoming travellers to a new province comes into view, those who keep their eyes peeled for it may spot an unmarked road that intersects with the north side of the highway about 300 metres east of the boundary. This is the beginning of a short drivable stretch of old highway that immediately turns westward, roughly parallel to the present TCH. Heading down this neglected road, keen eyes will make out the spot where the white double lines down the middle of the worn pavement change to yellow. This change marks the provincial boundary.

In the bush to the north of this spot and within sight of the road stands a large boulder. A blank, flat, rectangular portion of its surface indicates the place where a plaque has been pried away. Closer inspection will reveal the remains of flagpole bases to the rock's right and left. Decades have passed since the days when families stopped at a turnout on the opposite side of the road to have their pictures taken at this now-abandoned spot.

It is possible to drive a few metres into Manitoba on this old road, but no farther. Not only is nature reasserting its presence but human intervention has made sure that the road has been rendered completely impassable for any who might imagine they can use it as an alternate route into Manitoba's Whiteshell Provincial Park. Drivers simply have to retrace the short route to the present TCH, wondering perhaps whatever happened to that missing plaque.

Clark Saunders

Above: The welcome sign at the Manitoba-Ontario boundary.

Opposite: Old No. 1 crosses the Lockport Dam north of Winnipeg, where pelicans sometimes cool themselves on hot days.

Opposite: Stan Milosovic

Both images: Clark Saunders

The Travel Manitoba
Centre (top). The
plaque, now next to
the centre's door, once
graced a boulder on
the old highway.

Back on the new highway and just east of the map-shaped
sign announcing the route's arrival in Manitoba, a change in
the pavement marks the exact spot where a new jurisdiction
begins. Just past the Travel Manitoba centre on the right, an
exit leads to the centre's parking lot. A map near the southeast corner of the parking lot provides a useful orientation
to the neighbourhood. From here, steps lead up to the tourist information building. But before going inside, visitors
should have a look at the plaque to the left of the door. So
that's where it went! Yes, it's the plaque that was originally
mounted on the boulder at the provincial boundary on the
old highway. Even in its new location, it serves as a reminder
that a road of sorts joined the two provinces as part of a
national route as far back as 1932. On July 1 of that year (the 65th
anniversary of Confederation), the Manitoba-Ontario section of
the Trans-Canada Highway was officially opened for the benefit
of the more intrepid travellers of the day. (They may have called it
a highway, but in those days it was more like a track through the
woods. Motorists travelling between Kenora and Winnipeg generally allowed a day for the journey.)

Opposite the west end of the parking lot exit a road leads westward. This is another section of old highway. Drivers can follow it
if they like, but a dead end sign will soon come into view announcing that this bit of highway—like the bit that spans the boundary—is about to become undrivable.

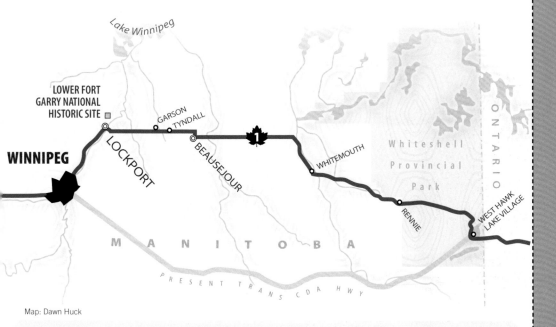

eastern manitoba

Lake Winnipeg

LOWER FORT GARRY NATIONAL HISTORIC SITE

WINNIPEG

LOCKPORT

GARSON

TYNDALL

BEAUSEJOUR

1

WHITEMOUTH

Whiteshell Provincial Park

RENNIE

WEST HAWK LAKE VILLAGE

ONTARIO

M A N I T O B A

PRESENT TRANS CDA HWY

Map: Dawn Huck

UNTIL THE MID-1950S THE NO. 1 HIGHWAY IN EASTERN MANITOBA FOLLOWED A LONGER AND MORE NORTHERLY ROUTE THAN IT DOES TODAY. MOST OF THE OLD ROUTE NOW BEARS THE NUMBER 44.

MANITOBA PROVINCIAL FLOWER

PRAIRE CROCUS

Stan Milosovic

Pulsatilla ludoviciana, also known as the pasque-flower, anemone patens or wind-flower, was adopted as Manitoba's floral emblem in 1906 following suggestions by the Manitoba Horticultural Society. Flower species were then voted on by Manitoba schoolchildren, who chose the prairie crocus first, while second place went to the prairie lily (now Saskatchewan's floral symbol), with the wild rose (now Alberta's provincial flower) third.

Clark Saunders

Motorists who want to start their journey on the old highway properly will need to return to the present highway and drive about four kilometres into Manitoba. (Those who are more interested in "getting there" than enjoying the trip can stay on the modern Trans-Canada which, since the mid-1950s, has been the preferred route between the southern Whiteshell—and all points east—and Winnipeg.) After the TCH passes through a couple of very deep dips, the exit leading to the beginning of Provincial Trunk Highway 44 appears on the right. A couple of kilometres north on this road traffic comes to a T-junction at the village of West Hawk Lake. At this junction, Highway 44—in these parts also designated as the La Vérendrye Trail—adds the subtitle "Historic Highway No. 1." The provincial government has even provided extra signs that say so.

Ultimately the way forward leads west from the T-junction, but in order to get a sense of the old highway it is worth turning right at the "T" and driving about three kilometres east. Until 2012, vehicles travelling this short distance began by driving on broken pavement through the West Hawk town site. But in that year, a project was begun to improve the main street of the village with new pavement, neat curbing and traffic-calming features. However, even today, once through the town site and continuing east beyond Crescent Beach, travellers will encounter the broken pavement of yore.

Old No. 1 west of West Hawk Lake (now Highway 44) has been designated an historic highway by the Manitoba government (below). It is also part of the La Vérendrye Trail (above), which recalls the route of the 18th century fur trader.

A short jaunt leads to a red barrier and the parking area for the trail to Hunt Lake. Here a sign marks the end of Historic No. 1. Beyond the barrier, pavement of a sort—even more broken than the stuff today's motorists are permitted to drive across—stretches eastward toward nearby Ontario. It is not accessible to vehicles, but those who are game for a two-kilometre round-trip hike can explore it and see where it leads. (Spoiler alert: The terminus of this trail will be revealed before the end of this paragraph.) Although nature is coming into its own again, the double yellow line that once marked the middle of this stretch of old highway is still visible in places. The rising slope of the road eventually comes up against the bed of the modern highway. A short stretch of newer gravel allows pedestrians to parallel the new route until evidence of the old one emerges again—from under the new highway, as it were. Those who keep walking will pass the dead end sign referred to above and end up in the Travel Manitoba parking lot.

Motorists who feel frustrated in their efforts to get anywhere on the old highway

Peter St. John

Peter St. John

should be of good cheer. From the Hunt Lake trail parking lot they will be able to retrace their route westward and continue into new territory without let or hindrance. The journey now begins in earnest. But it is worth taking a moment to notice the old office building of the Crescent Beach Cottages ("CBC") and Motel opposite Crescent Beach in West Hawk Lake town site. Though other buildings on the property date from more recent times, this period piece speaks of an earlier era.

Across the road from the CBC a historic display deserves inspection. It tells of how the lake—Manitoba's deepest—was created by a meteor slamming into the earth. No less significant for travellers of the old road is the information that completion of the highway from Winnipeg to West Hawk Lake in 1932 opened up the area to cottage development. Road construction was facilitated by a Depression-era project called the Single Men's Relief Program. Just a year before the

West Hawk Lake is north of today's TCH, but the historic highway travelled along its shores.

fill 'er up

WE TENDED TO CALL THEM "FILLING STATIONS" back then, and the gasoline was measured in gallons—imperial gallons, that is. There was no such thing as self-serve gas stations; the "ping, ping" of the signal bell as you drove over the cable was intended to announce your arrival and summon assistance. The attendant (usually male) wore a uniform that on a good day might include a cap.

"Mr. B/A", who made his advertising debut in 1957, was an idealized, cap-wearing employee. Smiling from magazine ads of the time, he even greeted customers with a salute. Whether his real-life counterparts saluted seems doubtful. But at least they would offer to check your oil and clean the windshield of bugs and other adhesions. (The bugs on the grill or bug-catcher you would have to attend to yourself.)

White Rose was just one of a number of brands that came and went with the oil company mergers and takeovers of the 20th century. Starting in 1901 as the Canadian Oil Refining Company in Petrolia, Ontario, within seven years the new venture was already in American hands. Later, the American parent company sold it to Nesbitt, Thompson and Company of Montreal. The White Rose logo first appeared on the company's signs in 1938. In the 1950s, White Rose, with filling stations in every province except British Columbia, was almost entirely Canadian owned. Then, early in the 1960s, another foreign-based enterprise, Shell (as in Royal Dutch Shell) Canada, gobbled the company up and the White Rose signs disappeared.

A similar fate befell the company represented by Mr. B/A. British American also began as a Canadian business and at one time even had subsidiaries in the United States. But after the Second World War, Gulf Oil began acquiring an interest in the company and by 1956 had gained control. In the early 1960s, Gulf took over two other Canadian oil companies—Purity 99 and Royalite. The old signs gradually disappeared and "Gulf" took their place.

The B/A logo, by the way, was meant to represent reversing oil droplets. The metal signs that would swing from their poles in a strong wind began to be replaced in 1954 when internally illuminated signs were introduced. B/A was also one of the first companies to provide road maps for its customers. The company started doing that back in 1929. Imperial Esso followed six years later.

The story of the Imperial Oil Company follows a now familiar course. Starting as a Canadian company, it was later acquired by Standard Oil, the enterprise created by John D. Rockefeller. Abbreviated as "S.O.", when spelled phonetically it came out as "Esso". By

Both images: Clark Saunders

the 1960s, the company had made a splash on both sides of the border with the advertising slogan, "Put a tiger in your tank."

Though it had a Canadian subsidiary, Texaco (founded as the Texas Fuel Company) was another oil company headquartered in our great neighbour to the south. Like other filling stations, Texaco came up with names for its regular and premium gasolines. Texaco called them "Fire Chief" and "Sky Chief", while B/A had its "88" and "98".

And then there was the challenge of getting the word out. Oil companies resorted not only to print media but to radio and television sponsorships as a means of advertising. In the United States, Texaco took over sponsorship of the Saturday afternoon Metropolitan Opera radio broadcasts in 1940 and continued in that role until it merged with Chevron in 2004. The Canadian Broadcasting Corporation began carrying these broadcasts in the 1930s and continued to do so after Texaco became involved.

Esso targeted a different audience. Imperial Esso had already been sponsoring radio hockey broadcasts for years when Hockey Night in Canada came to television in 1952 and just kept going. For 16 years, actor Murray Westgate was "your friendly Esso dealer" in the familiar cap wishing viewers, "Happy motoring."

Some gas companies, like White Rose, have vanished from the scene, but others, including Shell, remain. Gas pumps are still with us—only the design (and the prices!) have changed.

Peter St. John

Above: Old No. 1 travels through Whiteshell Provincial Park.

Below: Rennie, Manitoba, has no illusions about its place in the world.

highway reached this spot the provincial government had set aside the region as the Whiteshell Forest Preserve.

After reaching the T-junction, the old highway continues westward on what is now not just Historic Number 1 but Highway 44 as it heads through more of what is now known as the Whiteshell Provincial Park. Just beyond the edge of the town site Provincial Road 301 leads off to the left. Until the modern TCH provided more direct access from Winnipeg, people who built cottages at Falcon Lake would come as far as West Hawk on the old highway and then almost double back on this road to their summer retreats.

The rocky Canadian Shield country through which Highway 44 makes its way is dotted with marsh and lily ponds and can include sightings of deer, bear and beaver. As for the road, tinges of blue or red in successive stretches of pavement suggest that its surface dates from a variety of periods. No matter its hue, the road is shoulderless and, though it shows signs of having been improved over the years, its surface hardly rises above the level of the surrounding terrain.

WELCOME TO RENNIE
HOME OF SOMETHING
OR SOMEBODY FAMOUS...
SOMEDAY... MAYBE...

Clark Saunders

Just east of Rennie, where Provincial Road 307 heads off to the right and the northern Whiteshell (taking the La Vérendrye Trail with it), the pavement widens and acquires shoulders. Rennie is a tiny place remembered by generations of campers for its fire lookout tower and appreciated today for its disarmingly frank welcome sign: WELCOME TO RENNIE—HOME OF SOMETHING ... OR SOMEBODY FAMOUS ... SOMEDAY ... MAYBE ...

Both Images: Clark Saunders

The pavement improves again just before Whitemouth at the junction with southbound Highway 11. With dramatic suddenness, the Shield country gives way to the prairie. Travellers are advised to get used to it because there is more than a mile or two of it ahead.

The exit into Whitemouth at the eastern approach to the town leads almost immediately across the rough pavement of an older and more primitive version of the highway that runs parallel to the modern Number 44. A drive through the middle of the town passes, on the far side, the modern version of First Stop Groceries. You can't miss the long mural painted on the side of it depicting the old store and other local scenes from an earlier era. The loop through town rejoins the highway just before it passes historic Christ Church (Anglican) complete with old farm machinery from the ephemeral age of steam scattered around the churchyard.

As it heads northwest from Whitemouth Highway 44 doubles as Highway 11 until the latter declares its independence and leads north to Winnipeg River country. Shortly after the split, those who stay on Highway 44 will be reminded by a road sign that they are still on Historic No. 1. An older rendition of the Trans-Canada can be seen running parallel to No. 44 on the north side of the highway. Now a service road, this section runs all the way to Beausejour with a brief interruption at Seddons Corner, where the westbound lanes of Highway 44 widen and

Above: A portion of a mural on the side of First Stop Groceries in Whitemouth.

Below: A plaque marks the centenary of the creation of Christ Church in Whitemouth.

CHRIST CHURCH
WHITEMOUTH
THIS ANGLICAN CHURCH WAS
T IN 1905 BY THE PARISHIONERS FROM
LY DONATED MATERIALS ON DONATED LAND
GINALLY DEDICATED AUGUST 22nd 1905
IN SERVICE UNTIL DECEMBER 1995
DICATED THIS 11th DAY OF SEPTEMBER 2005
COMMEMORATING THIS CHURCH'S
0th ANNIVERSARY AND THE CENTENNIAL
HE RURAL MUNICIPALITY OF WHITEMOUTH
EMOUTH MUNICIPAL MUSEUM SOCIETY

displace it just before the intersection. The older highway is drivable although the pavement west of Seddons Corner is not up to the same standard as that to the east. At the Brokenhead River, just before Beausejour, an old low-profile truss bridge parallels a newer bridge on the present highway.

Approaching Beausejour, the modern highway splits and the westbound lanes once more jog to the right and displace the old highway. Drivers should not let this distract them from noticing the tall cowboy on the period-piece drive-in sign on approaching the junction with Highway 12. Here, there is a choice to be made.

Some may choose to turn right, bypassing the town. A mile to the north this route turns left as Highway 44 and continues westward. In the 1950s, summertime Sunday evenings saw traffic jams at this second intersection as cars coming south from the beaches on the east side of Lake Winnipeg merged with traffic returning to Winnipeg from the Whiteshell. By the 1960s, the problem had been alleviated. Highway 59 through Libau had been paved, thus diverting beach traffic onto a more direct homeward route from Lake Winnipeg, while vehicles from the southern Whiteshell were able to use the new TCH.

The other option—and a more interesting one—is to continue westward on approaching Beausejour, entering the town on what

A vintage cowboy sign greets visitors just east of Beausejour, while the town's Lyric Theatre, its signage bright and appealing, is still open for business though many small-town cinemas are gone.

Peter St. John

Clark Saunders

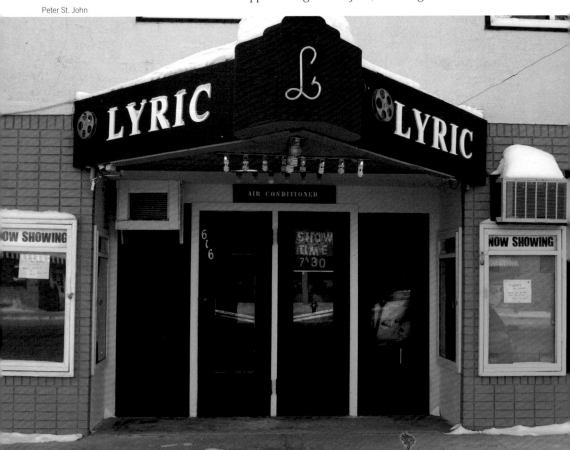

Both Images: Peter St. John

becomes its main drag. This is the highway's older route and passes the vintage Lyric Theatre, built in 1944.

The historic highway signs indicate a right turn at First Street. A mile's drive leads to a reunion with Highway 44 north of town. Turning left here, the route continues westward on what is now a modern four-lane highway. After passing Tyndall, the town for which a famous variety of limestone is named, an older (but not ancient) highway diverges from the present one on the left. It is worth joining this route when the opportunity presents itself—as it does more than once. It passes blocks of Tyndall stone stacked by the roadside and, closer to Garson, quarries from which such noble edifices as the Canadian Parliament Buildings and the Manitoba Legislative Building were constructed. Until the 1990s, traffic followed this route right through Garson and past its eponymous hotel, now done over but still standing where it has always been.

West of Garson, there is an opportunity to return to the modern Highway 44. It is best to take it. After the cloverleaf interchange with Highway 59 comes a broad stretch of road that bears little resemblance to what motorists would have encountered 50 or 60 years ago. But after crossing the Red River Floodway, dating from the 1960s, the route arrives at the village of Lockport, which, though changed in many ways, continues to offer a number of familiar landmarks. The hotel, now modernized, still stands at the corner of Henderson Highway (Provincial Road 204).

Before crossing the bridge directly ahead, those who make a left

Old No. 1 passes both Tyndall and Garson, where beautiful limestone used in many of Canada's public buildings is quarried. Famous for its creamy colour, Tyndall Stone often contains fossils of ancient sea creatures, such as the half-billion-year-old Ordovician cephalopod (inset).

turn onto this provincial road will soon find themselves at the Half Moon Drive In. The old restaurant with its row of three signature half-moon-shaped roofs is gone, and the new restaurant is not on the same site exactly, but it has effectively recreated '50s kitsch in its decor. Until 2011, two tall, skinny gas pumps—the kind that could still be found functioning at filling stations in the early postwar years—stood guard at the north end of the parking lot. With their trademark "Half Moon" insignia, they can still be found depicted in a mural inside the restaurant. The same mural includes a representation of the old drive-in with cars of the 1950s and three icons of the period—James Dean, Marilyn Monroe and Elvis Presley—looking as if they all decided to drop in for a bite on the same day. The two White Rose gas pumps just inside the west entrance are worth a look, too. Like their taller brothers in the mural, they are topped with globes. They come complete with quaint dials for measuring fuel.

Back at Highway 44, the old route continues west, crossing the Red River on the bridge of the St. Andrew's Lock and Dam. Opened in 1910 to ease river traffic over a series of rapids, the structure underwent a major overhaul in 1993 but still looks much as it did a hundred years ago. Today the boats that use the locks are more likely to be pleasure craft than commercial vessels, but in summer anglers can be seen fishing the downstream waters as they have for generations.

Peter St. John

The old gas pump (above) stood outside the Half Moon Drive In in Lockport until 2011, but St. Andrew's Lock and Dam bides eternal.

Clark Saunders

Both Images: Peter St. John

On the far side stands Skinner's, the establishment that answers the challenge thrown out by the Half Moon Drive In. In fact, it should be the other way around, because the older of the two Skinner's Restaurant locations dates back to 1929. The café on Highway 44 (the newer of the two) was originally built after the western approach to the bridge was redesigned in 1946. For the older location turn left (south) off the Highway and backtrack east on Stevens Avenue to the river. Here, on River Road (Provincial Road 238), in the shadow of the bridge, those in search of a few carbs will find the original location of Skinner's—"Home of the World Famous Hot Dog". (A Pepsi-Cola sign proclaims: "Worth a dime—costs a nickel.") Most of the items on the old menus will look familiar. But what is a "nip"? you ask. Well, in these parts it was the local patois for "hamburger"; the term was popularized by Winnipeg's Salisbury House chain of restaurants.

Those with an interest in earlier history may choose to head south toward the city on the River Road with its old houses and St. Andrew's Church reminding travellers of the early decades of the Red River Settlement. (Today you can even enjoy the pavement, but don't forget that drivers in the middle of the last century had to make do with gravel.) Others might want to stop in at Lower Fort Garry National Historic Site. To reach this—the flagship of the

At Skinner's, the '50s is alive and well with wall-mounted boxes in every booth, all connected to a jukebox that plays blasts from the past, while the walls are a hockey hall of fame displaying former glories. Memorabilia include reminders of food and drink prices of yesteryear.

Both Images: Peter St. John

Above: St. Andrew's Church (above), the oldest stone church in Western Canada, was begun in 1845 and 1849 and is still in use today.

Below: The governor's residence at Lower Fort Garry NHS (as it is today). Midcentury visitors would have found it leased to a private club.

federal government's historic sites in Western Canada—it is best to return from the older Skinner's to Highway 44 and follow it a few hundred metres west until it ends at the T-junction with Highway 9. (Have a good look at the Historic Highway No. 1 sign, because you shall not see its like again.) By turning right, drivers will arrive in less than five minutes at the Lower Fort. Since the mid-'60s the federal government has done a lot to bring the place to life and give an impression of the way things were in the days of the fur trade. But for much of the 20th century—until 1963, in fact—the Hudson's Bay Company had given a long-term lease to a golf course and motor country club. The lessees prettied the place up with lawns and flowerbeds. Although the HBC handed the place over to the Feds in 1951, it was only after the country club lease ran out that Parks Canada could get to work rooting out the anachronistic flowerbeds and restoring the place to its 19th-century appearance.

For those who have included Lower Fort Garry in their itinerary—and for those who have not—the onward route is south (or, in Red River terms, upstream) via Highway 9 to Winnipeg. The area north of the city is much more built up than it used to be, but on the east side of the highway on the approach to Middlechurch, the road passes a series of cemeteries that have been there for a long time, each catering to the deceased of its own particular religious persua-

Stan Milosovic Collection

sion. And on the other (west) side of the road, watch for the vintage metal signs that decorate the walls of the old yellow brick building that is now the home of Candle Company Antiques, a business that takes its name from an actual candle factory that occupied the premises in earlier days.

By the time it crosses over the Perimeter Highway, the route has become Winnipeg's Main Street. As late as the 1960s, Greater Winnipeg could claim to be Canada's fourth largest city. In those days, roughly half the population of the metropolis lived in suburbs such as Old Kildonan and West Kildonan through which Main Street passes. (These areas were amalgamated into a "unicity" in 1972.) Kildonan Park, on the east side of Main Street, has been around for more than a hundred years, but an addition of the '50s was the outdoor summer theatre, Rainbow Stage. In its early years bench-type seating predominated and inclement weather could send patrons scurrying for the sheltered areas along the sides of the open-air auditorium—or lead to outright cancellations of performances. Since those far-off days, the theatre has come to enjoy the security of a domed roof and the quality of a much-improved sound system—not to mention production values that make sitting "under the rainbow" a much different experience from the one that greeted the first generation of theatre-goers.

Until it closed at the end of 2012, travellers who passed up the opportunity to eat at Lockport could stop in at the Kelekis Restaurant at 1100 Main Street on the corner of Redwood. Known originally for

Dated 1943, this postcard shows the corner of Portage and Main, looking west, and complete with streetcars, which were eliminated in 1955.

Courtesy Of James Richardson & Sons, Ltd.

Travellers along Old No. 1 West would have found Winnipeg's fabled corner of Portage and Main rather different than it is today. Before the 34-storey International Style Richardson Building was built in 1969, the northeast corner was, for a time, adorned by a mock-Tudor filling station.

their chips (that's what we used to call "fries" in this country—and we were as likely to put vinegar on them as ketchup), the Kelekis family opened their establishment at this location in the 1940s and expanded it in 1955. The concept of take-out food was still fairly novel in those days and Kelekis was among the first places in this part of the world to introduce it.

North Main, as it approaches downtown, is a mixture of old and new. In the old days the underpass beneath the CPR tracks was as impressive as the Grand Canyon for children who had never seen topography more exciting that the flattest of prairies. Among the more recent features are the Centennial Concert Hall and the Manitoba Museum (dating from the late '60s), which have made a fine addition to the city's amenities. But across the street stands the undistinguished city hall—a matter for regret, for it replaced a quaint Victorian gingerbread building that is now lost forever.

Despite the impact of developers, downtown Winnipeg still includes a number of impressive buildings that date from the pre-First World War period. At Portage and Main—a corner perhaps better known across the country a half century ago than it is today—three of the corners are occupied by structures that did not exist until after 1965.

But on the southeast corner the Bank of Montreal building (1913) expresses something of the amazing confidence this city exuded in its youth—amazing especially when one considers that 40 years before this building was constructed the street it stands on was a muddy ox track running through a rough-and-ready, makeshift village.

Opposite: Stan Milosovic

from
WINNIPEG
~ to the SASKATCHEWAN
BORDER

Heading west from the iconic intersection of Portage and Main, imagine what it would have been like to share Portage Avenue with Winnipeg's streetcars. That is what motorists had to do until the city's fleet was sold off in 1955.

This part of the downtown area now includes a mixture of the new and the old. Some of Winnipeg's grand old buildings have fallen to the wrecker's ball, but others remain. The white façade of the Childs Building is gone, but the former home of Birks Jewellers with its terracotta walls and distinctive frieze is looking fresh these days. Eaton's is no more, its spot being occupied by the MTS Centre, but The Bay limps along on half of its six floors. The face of downtown Winnipeg has been significantly altered—and not necessarily for the better—by the Portage Place shopping mall. At any rate, it isn't easy to conjure up an image of the city centre as it was before 1965.

A few blocks west of The Bay, Broadway merges from the left. Since the completion of the present TCH between the Whiteshell and Winnipeg in the 1950s, motorists entering the city from the east have followed a newer through-town route that deposits traffic from Broadway onto Portage Avenue at this point. From here westward through the rest of the city the new route is identical with the old. Mind you, since about 1960 motorists who have had no need to stop in Winnipeg have opted to bypass the city entirely by taking Perimeter Highway south (Highway 100) around its southern outskirts.

Anyone travelling through the city and in the mood for a meal

PORTAGE AVENUE. WINNIPEG.

Stan Milosovic Collection

Above: Portage Avenue, looking east toward The Bay in the early 1950s.

Opposite: A wintry day near the Manitoba-Saskatchewan border, harkening back to the landscape of the middle of the 20th century.

Clark Saunders

Above: No sushi at Rae
and Jerry's on Portage
Avenue in 1957. And
none now.

Below: street art in
pre-Banksy times.

Peter St. John

that is a bit more up-market than hotdogs, hamburgers and chips should keep an eye out for Rae and Jerry's Steak House. It has been at its present location, on the north side of the avenue four kilometres west of Portage and Main, since 1957. The sign itself will prepare diners for what they will find as they step through the door: a period piece that has changed little over the years and offers excellent prime rib served by uniformed career waitresses amid a décor that favours the colour red. (Those who somehow miss Rae and Jerry's should watch for the Silver Heights Restaurant 3½ kilometres farther on; it opened in the same year.)

Just past Rae and Jerry's, Portage Avenue passes Polo Park. Dating from the same period as the two aforementioned restaurants, Winnipeg's first major shopping centre replaced the racetrack of the same name, which in turn replaced the original polo field. The shopping centre has undergone major facelifts since its inauguration. One of the first changes involved covering in the area between the rows of stores. Call it a mall now if you like; the term post-dates its early years.

Five kilometers west of Polo Park and just past the major intersection with Moray Street, a longtime landmark can be seen on the right at the corner of Aldine Street. The storey-and-a-half cartoon of a tall, thin hobo painted on the side of a building is accompanied by the caption, "It's a Long Tramp." Restored in 1994, the tramp first appeared in the 1920s. Some things have changed since then. When it was first constructed, the building it decorates was well out of the city. For many years it was the home of a drug store but now houses a leather jacket business. And the words that complete the pun—"54 miles to Portage"— refer to the distance west on the modern highway to Portage La Prairie. The trip on the old highway—the one midcentury travellers would have taken—is a bit longer.

This part of Winnipeg has little to offer in the way of hostelries that date back to the early postwar decades, although the two-storey Boulevard Motel with its vintage sign on the south side of the road at 3120 Portage Avenue gives a sense of the era. Across the street at 3095 stands a landmark of greater distinction. When

western manitoba

Map: Dawn Huck

IN THE EARLY POSTWAR YEARS, THE HIGHWAY'S ROUTE VARIED IN MANY PLACES FROM THE PRESENT ONE. BETWEEN WHITE HORSE PLAIN AND PORTAGE LA PRAIRIE IT RAN NORTH OF THE ASSINIBOINE RIVER RATHER THAN SOUTH OF IT. EAST AND WEST OF CARBERRY IT RAN SOUTH OF THE PRESENT ROUTE. WEST OF BRANDON IT SIMPLY FOLLOWED A ZIGZAG PATTERN BASED ON SECTION LINES.

MANITOBA PROVINCIAL TREE

WHITE SPRUCE

Peter St. John

Picea glauca, as botanists know the white spruce, was proclaimed Manitoba's provincial tree in 1991. A long-lived conifer, with exceptional trees living 300 years, it grows in almost every region of the province and can reach 30 metres (or 100 feet) in height. White spruce are used for construction and for Christmas trees, and their long, flexible surface roots were used for millennia to "sew" or bind birchbark to canoe frames.

Clark Saunders

Wherever cars went fast food followed. A&W restaurants were among the first to capitalize on the growing trend. Though remodelled several times, the A&W (above) in west Winnipeg keeps a photo gallery of the old days and is a home-away-from-the-garage to a classic car club.

Headingley's Nick's Inn (at right) was a similarly classic drive'n'dine destination.

an A&W restaurant first rose on this spot in the mid-'50s, it was the first of the chain to appear in Canada. It is still in business. The structure has undergone changes over the years but its interior walls display photographs that recall its early days, and members of a classic car club show up regularly to add to the sense of time warp.

West of the Perimeter Highway the speed limit is 70 kilometres per hour. In pre-metric days it was 45 mph, and those who exceeded it often found themselves paying a fine. Nowadays the stretch that leads to Headingley is built up almost all the way, but 50 or 60 years ago the place had more of the feeling of a distinct village. Two landmarks that evoke those earlier days are, on the right, the black-and-white Holy Trinity Anglican Church with its distinctive tower (the present tower is a reasonable facsimile of the original), and, on the left, Nick's Inn restaurant. The latter has been an institution since Greek immigrant Nick Cholakis bought the place in 1963.

Just beyond Headingley—and just before the weigh station—comes an opportunity to head off onto the old highway. Here it runs along on the right and parallels the new highway as a frontage road. Almost immediately it passes—on the left and over toward the Assiniboine River—what is now the Headingley Correctional Centre. Years ago, it was known simply as Headingley Gaol. Gaol Road preserves the quaint spelling.

Travellers who keep their eyes peeled can soon spot a cairn beside the road on the right. (Those who have stayed on the highway will have another chance to access the frontage road just before it

Both Images: Peter St. John

reaches the cairn.) This marks the Principal Meridian of the Dominion Land Survey System. The first marker from which the section lines across the prairies were measured was set half a mile to the south of this spot in 1871. It was these same section lines that would determine the location of most of the region's first roads, including the roads that would serve as the first cross-country route through much of the area.

The frontage road comes to a stop sign just beyond the point where Highway 26 leaves the present Trans-Canada or Number 1 Highway to follow the north side of the Assiniboine to Portage la Prairie. Highway 26 is the old Number 1. To follow it, drivers need to turn right here. (Those who have stayed on the main highway have an opportunity to exit onto Highway 26 at this point.) In the "V" between the old highway and the new, a statue of a white horse stands vigil, commemorating an Aboriginal legend. The plaques describing the story and other aspects of the early history of the area, known traditionally as White Horse Plain, date from 1966.

The new highway, by the way, runs more or less parallel to the CNR main line (to the south), while from the old highway it may be possible to make out the CPR main line off to the north. The two lines cross at Portage La Prairie. From there it is the CNR that takes the more northerly route, heading eventually for Saskatoon and Edmonton, while the CPR blazes the trail that would eventu-

From this plaque west of Headingley, which is affixed to a prominent stone cairn, all section lines across the prairies were measured.

ally be followed by the Trans-Canada Highway. The Winnipeg-to-Portage stretch of the present TCH dates from the late 1950s. Almost immediately after its divergence from the old highway (now Highway 26), westbound traffic crosses the Assiniboine River on a bridge that was constructed near—but not over—the river. The river was then diverted under it. An oxbow is all that is left of the river's original route.

The new highway provides access to three campgrounds that have connections to the early days of the modern route. The site of Sunny Harbour, opposite the White Horse Monument, has been turned into a residential area, but Welcomestop is close by and may be considered the old campground's successor. Just before re-crossing the Assiniboine closer to Portage, the four-lane highway passes Creek-side Camping and RV Park on the south side of the road. Now a privately run enterprise, until the 1980s this was the site of Norquay Provincial Park. By the early 1960s, families were camping here and splashing around at Scotty's Beach. A little farther on and on the opposite side of the road is Miller's Camping Resort. This venerable spot has gone through several owners and a name change or two, but it dates back to the early days of this stretch of the present highway.

But for those who chose the old highway back at White Horse Plain, the route follows Highway 26 for a short distance before ar-

The White Horse Monument, symbolizing an Aboriginal legend, marks the place where Old No. 1 turns north-west toward the Village of St. François Xavier, a Franco-Manitoban community.

Peter St. John

Peter St. John

riving at St. François Xavier. Known to anglophones as St. Francis, the village, with its associations with 19th century Métis leader Cuthbert Grant, is an old one. It is still distinguished by its Roman Catholic Church. In terrain where the presence of one or more grain elevators has usually guided travellers to a town, here the central spire of the church announces the location of the village for some distance around.

Already motorists will be enjoying a more interesting landscape than the one that surrounds the new highway. Here the Assiniboine is on the left. Even when you can't actually see it—or the dikes that sometimes border it—the trees that mark its route bring relief from endless prairie. Mind you, the prairie to the north is worthy of note, too. This is the rich soil of the Portage Plains. The sights you think you see may be only a mirage. But there is no mistaking the plethora of red-winged blackbirds or the sound of meadowlarks. Those who are really lucky may even be able to watch a hawk making lazy circles in the sky.

There are distinctive old buildings, too, like St. Paul's Anglican Church, which has stood alone by the roadside for more than a hundred years. At Poplar Point, about a half-hour drive northwest of St. François Xavier along Highway 26, are found a post office and a curling rink that likewise were there long before midcentury motorists drove past them. Located south of the highway just west of Provincial Road 430, St. Anne's Anglican Church was up and running a half-century before St. Paul's. In fact, the present building marked its centenary as far back as 1964.

Above: A rainbow can transform the flat prairie landscape.

Below: A male Red Winged Blackbird collecting seeds from an outdoor feeding station in Manitoba.

Canstockphoto/CSP - 11584123

Clark Saunders

a motel BY ANY OTHER NAME

WHEN BABY BOOMERS AND THEIR PARENTS TOOK TO THE OPEN ROAD in the postwar years, some carried camping equipment, while others pulled trailers. But it is probably safe to say that most stayed at motels. Certainly that's what our family did.

In the early years, when the roads were poor and travellers were few, most roadside accommodations consisted of groups of detached cabins. As time went on, some of these businesses took to calling themselves tourist camps or motor courts, auto courts or bungalows. But eventually the preferred term became a contraction of "motor hotels": motels. With the term came the style: a row of attached units, each with its own door to the outside world and a spot for a car to park right in front of it. It was the kind of place Norman Bates (of *Psycho* fame) attended to when he was not preoccupied with taxidermy. (Significantly, the Bates Motel was on an old bypassed highway.) Air conditioning was virtually unknown in these motels; likewise "non-smoking units". And in an age when many families saved money by doing much of their own cooking, kitchenettes were common. Television, on the other hand, was a rarity until the mid-1950s, and even then it came only in black and white.

Most motels were privately owned; this was before the age of chains like Super 8, Travelodge and Holiday Inn where the standard hardly varies from one town to another. My parents generally asked to see the room—and check out the beds—before making a commitment.

Later refinements included the addition of swimming pools—outdoor ones, at least—at some of the swankier places. After a day's journey in the hot summer sun in a car with no air conditioning, the kids would be begging to stay at such a luxurious establishment. A two-storey arrangement, still with outside access to each unit, was the mark of a newer enterprise. And the later use of the full term—"motor hotel"—seemed to indicate up-market aspirations on the part of the management.

And the cost of staying in a motel? My recollection is that in the mid-'50s nine or 10 dollars could get you decent accommodations for a family of five. By 1960, rates for a similar place with a pool had risen to $12 or $15. The cheapest place I can ever remember staying was on the North Hill in Brandon. It was a cabin consisting of one large room with curtains separating the sagging beds from one another. The rate was $7, and it wasn't worth a penny more.

Sweet Dreams Motel in Broadview, Saskatchewan, is typical of the style of accommodation available in the 1950s and early 1960s.

Stan Milosovic

All good things come to an end, and that is what Highway 26 does just before Portage la Prairie. You can follow it as it makes a sharp left turn and leads back onto Highway 1, but there is the option of going straight ahead as the pavement continues on what is still the old route. A kilometre farther west a jog to the left connects with Highway 1A—the old highway through town, known in these parts as Saskatchewan Avenue. Some may choose to stop at the Fort la Reine Museum (named for the structure built by La Vérendrye in the area) but though the buildings gathered together here are undoubtedly old, this project was just a gleam in Portage la Prairie's eye until the late 1960s.

Portage itself boasts many fine old buildings. A left turn at the impressive city hall leads within a few blocks to the bridge that crosses a lake (really an oxbow) to Island Park. Well, it's not really an island either. But if the weather is warm those who remembered

Bucolic countryside near Poplar Point.

Clark Saunders

to pack a picnic lunch will be glad they did. And they will be following the example of many travellers of yesteryear.

Back on the old route through town Portage has a few vintage motels on offer. The Westgate Inn was passed on the way into town. The Midtown Inn—another two-storey establishment, suggesting that it appeared late in the period—comes up on the left. Just before what was the western edge of town (until the malls and fast-food outlets extended the outer limits), two other contenders can be found. There is the Hi Way Motel on the right. But just before it comes the sign pointing left to the Yellow Quill. A quiet half-block off the old highway, it has stood its ground for more than half a century. And for those who blinked and missed all these opportunities, one more—the Sunset Motel—awaits the wandering traveller in what was countryside when it was built. An access road running parallel to the highway on its south side is an alignment of the old road. It runs right by the Sunset before turning to gravel and petering out to avoid colliding with the cloverleaf that reunites the modern bypass with the old through-town route.

This marks the end of Highway 1A. From here the new highway has in effect been laid down on top of the old and runs nearly as straight as a die westward for close to 30 kilometres. In the process it says good-bye to the Yellowhead Highway (Highway 16, formerly Highway 4) which heads north and eventually west and provides another route to the coast. This section of the No. 1 also passes—on its south side just beyond Provincial Road 242—the lonely tree that some say marks the midpoint between Winnipeg and Brandon.

The modern highway bypasses the towns along the way, but there are a couple of opportunities to follow the old route at MacGregor and at Austin. At MacGregor, the exit brings traffic to the Service Road South, an older version of the highway—a road that skirts the northern edge of town. There is an opportunity to return to the modern Trans-Canada just west of MacGregor. Then the Austin exit follows the old route right through that town. Aside from these loops the present TCH follows pretty closely a route that dates back beyond the '50s, though needless to say people didn't have the luxury of four lanes in those days.

Since the early 1950s, many tourists have taken the time to drive three kilometres south on Highway 34 just west of Austin to the Manitoba Agricultural Museum, which is dedicated to preserving a living record of early farming life and work in this part of the world. The highlight of the museum's year continues to be the annual Threshermen's Reunion and Stampede held in the last week of July.

Alex Campbell / Courtesy Of The Manitoba Agricultural Museum

After Sidney, travellers interested in driving a stretch of old highway should watch for Provincial Road 251 and the sign to Melbourne. Sixteen kilometers (that's an even 10 miles in old money) on this section of old TCH will bring motorists to Carberry, and another 16 will bring them back to the modern highway. This is one of those winding, hilly sections of old highway that runs along right down on the ground with little in the way of built-up foundation or shoulders. The terrain is pleasant and varied; Spirit Sands (or the Carberry Sandhills) and Spruce Woods Provincial Park lie not far to the south. At Carberry, the road passes through town just north of its commercial centre. None of the businesses on this route are as old as the '60s but motorists who stay on the modern highway and find themselves passing the Robin's Nest Motel (five kilometres north of town at the corner of the TCH and Highway 5) will see in it a reminder of the era.

The provincial road completes its winding route by rejoining today's Highway Number 1 east of Douglas. This little town was already bypassed by 1950. In the 1930s and '40s, the main road came down the hill from the north, made a sharp right (which some motorists missed, though they realized their error almost immediately) and followed the main street west through town. Taking the Douglas exit is the way to check out this route today, but drivers should be prepared to backtrack to the highway rather than continuing west on that main street. The pavement ends after it leaves town.

Next is Western Manitoba's largest urban area: Brandon. Until the

Above: The Village Street at the Manitoba Agricultural Museum west of Austin. The museum preserves machinery and buildings from the pioneer period.

Spirit Sands, south of the TCH, is the remains of an ancient glacial spillway.

Peter St. John

Stan Milosovic

Sometimes called the halfway tree, this century-old Manitoba cottonwood, a lonely sentinel in the landscape, is said to mark the midpoint between Winnipeg and Brandon.

late 1950s, the TCH came to a stop here at a T-junction. Crossing its path was—and still is—the No. 10 Highway. Before the bypass was built, it would not have been possible to go forward on pavement from here. Instead, drivers needed to make a left turn and follow 1st Street down the hill. Today this is Highway 1A. Before making the turn, though (and you really should), it is worth taking note of Barney's Motel at the intersection of Highways 1 and 10. It dates back to the early days of the bypass.

The North Hill down which Highway 1A descends through Brandon used to be the site of a number of motels. The Midway is one of the last survivors of an earlier era. Farther down the hill and on the opposite side of the street, the Brandon Mental Health Centre still occupies its traditional site. Crossing the Assiniboine, the old route continues south until, at Victoria Avenue, Highway 1A turns westward and marks the southern edge of the city centre. This street with its distinctive central boulevard remains a mostly residential avenue featuring gracious character homes from an earlier era. By 18th Street motorists will have travelled a mile since turning west, because 1st and 18th Street mark section lines. Until the late '50s, those in search of an all-paved route to the West Coast might have turned left here and headed south on the Number 10 to the United States before continuing their westward travels.

Just after 18th Street, No. 1A passes the university. Sixty years ago there wasn't much of Brandon beyond this. Today, suburbs flank the through-town route as it heads due west and, after passing the vintage Casablanca Motor Inn, carries on through the countryside until it reaches the low-level underpass below the rail line at Kemnay. After all the warnings about over-height vehicles needing to take an alternate route, drivers may feel like ducking as they descend through this old, under-grade twist in the road.

Just beyond Kemnay, Highway 1A ends. The remains of old highway can be seen continuing a short distance westward, but its dead end will persuade travellers to join the TCH as it completes its bypass here. Those who have stayed on the No. 1 will have passed through the Assiniboine Valley at a spot where it justifies the local moniker, "Grand Valley". (When the CPR was built through the area, speculators bought up land, convinced that a town would arise

Old No. 1 travels through downtown Brandon, Manitoba's second-largest city, which has preserved many of its character buildings.

Abbeywood / www.en.wikipedia.org

Stan Milosovic

West of Brandon, the TCH passes through "Grand Valley," a section of the otherwise placid Assiniboine Valley favoured with especially attractive views. Unfortunately, in 2011, the valley attracted the waters of the flooding Assiniboine River.

in their midst. Prices were driven to such a fever pitch that the site of present-day Brandon was chosen instead.) The landscape here is much more dramatic than the territory downstream where the east-bound Assiniboine meanders modestly across the plains.

In the 1940s motorists heading from this point to the boundary with Saskatchewan and beyond were obliged to travel over gravel roads that followed section lines: a few miles west, then a mile north, then a few more miles west, then a couple of miles north, and so on. For a taste of this kind of route today's tourist should keep an eye out for Provincial Road 250. But instead of turning left onto the pavement, making a right turn onto the gravel will lead immediately to Provincial Road 455 heading west. This is the route motorists would have followed seventy years ago. The lack of pavement may seem trying at times, but when the dust settles the road provides some lovely vistas. At the T-junction at Highway 21 it will be a relief to be able to travel south on pavement, but the route is still following this ancient path. At Griswold it reaches the modern TCH, which keeps close to the old route from this point as far as Oak Lake.

The more faint-of-heart will have stayed on the No. 1 Highway as it heads toward Alexander. On its approach to the little town the new four-lane highway descends a modest incline. The remains of an earlier alignment with sharper turns lies to the south on this slope, but those driving east will find it easier to spot.

By the late 1940s, decision-makers had realized that the railway had got it right in the first place. Finally, a road was constructed that pretty much followed the same route as the present highway all the way to Regina, heading mostly west-by-north-west-ish and rarely passing out of sight of the CPR mainline. Mind you, highway builders of the 1950s would have been more intimidated by the topography and consequently would have included more twists and turns than today's broad version does. And the road would have gone through more towns in those days. We'll take note of some of these variations as we journey on.

As it happens, the next town to be encountered—Oak Lake—was the last in Western Manitoba to be bypassed. It is possible even now to leave the highway and drive though Oak Lake on what was still the TCH barely three decades ago. The present access road into town makes a 90-degree turn onto Main Street—the old highway. Disused portions of the old road can be seen stretching eastward and westward from the town and becoming overgrown. Closer to the CPR tracks, North Railway Street appears to be an even older alignment. In the 1940s, the gravel route ran north from here for a mile before it was confronted by the sudden appearance of the Assiniboine Valley and started zigzagging its way in a mostly westward direction toward Virden.

White-tailed deer, native to the northern Great Plains, are often seen, particularly in early morning and the evening. In the autumn, during the fall breeding period or rut, mature males like this handsome buck sometimes disrupt traffic as they pursue does across the highway.

USDA photo by Scott Bauer / www.en.wikipedia.org

Oil pump near Virden.

Photo courtesy of Tim Smith / Brandon Sun

Since shortly after 1950, when oil was discovered in the Virden district motorists have been alerted to the town's proximity by the appearance of bobbing oil pumps—the kind some of us described as "grasshoppers". Manitoba's oil fields expanded southward in later years, but Virden still lays claim to the title of the province's "oil capital". By the time prospectors had struck Texas tea the highway was already skirting the northern edge of the town. And although the western reaches of the province were the last to see the TCH twinned, there has been a short four-lane bit at Virden for many decades. On the south side of the highway at this point, the Country-side Inn and Virden Motel have been around for about as long as the divided highway.

During the Second World War, a gravel road still conveyed travellers by a series of right angles north from Virden and west to Hargrave (barely a spot on the map today), then north and west again to Elkhorn. At this, the last town of any size in Manitoba, the road that crosses the highway at a sharp angle from east to west is the old route. A little jog has been inserted to minimize the angle as it crosses into town where it becomes Richhill Avenue, Elkhorn's main street. It continues due west until it makes another right angle turn, this time heading north to Kirkella before running west into Saskatchewan. By 1950, all this had been replaced by a route that approximates the present one, making a smooth northwesterly approach to the neighbouring province. On departing from the keystone province motorists pass a Travel Manitoba information centre welcoming people driving in the opposite direction. They also pass a clone of the large Manitoba-shaped sign that welcomed them when they crossed into Manitoba from Ontario. At least it looks like Manitoba if you glance at it in your rearview mirror.

Opposite: Stan Milosovic

from the
SASKATCHEWAN
BORDER
- to REGINA

"The land is without character." Such was Edward McCourt's verdict on eastern Saskatchewan in his book, *The Road Across Canada*. Travelling the Trans-Canada Highway in 1963, he found the road excellent but the country dull. "Empty land. Empty sky. A stranger to the prairies feels uneasily that he is driving straight into infinity."

McCourt, a prolific writer and observer of prairie life in the postwar years, found the two-lane highway curving from time to time "for no apparent reason, except, perhaps, to counteract road hypnosis." Had he travelled the route a dozen or so years earlier, not only would he have been travelling on gravel, he would have been negotiating roads that ran even straighter. Until the early 1950s, the route tended to follow section lines as it did in Western Manitoba: a short distance straight north followed by a longer distance straight west in a zigzag series of 90-degree angles.

The road has changed since then. By McCourt's time curves had replaced corners, and pavement had superseded dirt and gravel. In the years since, a two-lane highway has become four-lane and bypass surgery has been performed on nearly every town.

But the terrain has not changed. This was and remains farmland. Although the Prairie provinces may be known for wheat, followed distantly by oats and rye, the farmscapes include the blue of flax in bloom and the yellow of mustard and its younger relative, canola—a variant of rapeseed. (Apart from the occasional crop of sunflowers, in the 1950s a yellow field would have been mustard; the canola came along later.) And, as we will see, those who venture off the modern highway and into some of Saskatchewan's little towns may encounter some pleasant surprises. The land, in short, may have more character than Edward McCourt perceived.

Above: *The Road Across Canada*, Edward McCourt's memoir of his cross-Canada road trip, published in 1965.

Opposite: In the late 1940s, travellers on Old No. 1 would have navigated gravel roads much like the one opposite.

Peter St. John

A yellow field on the prairies today is likely a crop of canola.

One town that remained unavoidable until long after McCourt drove the highway was Moosomin. The first sizeable town that greets westbound travellers after they enter Saskatchewan, Moosomin had until many years later a bypass that was not really a bypass at all. Cutting across the northeast corner of town it required drivers to reduce their speed as they passed businesses that catered to the travelling public.

Today a newer four-lane bypass (part of a 21st-century project that twinned the highway to the Manitoba boundary) skirts the same corner but at a greater distance from the town centre. The old route is still accessible, however. Although it dead-ends east of town, it can be accessed by the Moosomin exit at the eastern approach. Park Avenue—which is what it becomes when it enters the town itself— still runs by the Twi-Lite and Prairie Pride motels, both predating 1965. These venerable independent operations still compete with the newer, larger chains that face the modern bypass. And as the old bypass was being constructed at the end of the 1940s, a White Rose gas station was built at the corner of Park Avenue and Main. It's still there, but today it operates as a Shell station.

Those with long memories may recall a still older version of the highway. Until shortly after the Second World War a dirt road led east from Moosomin toward Fleming. In Moosomin itself it was Broadway, a street that still runs through the centre of town. From

eastern saskatchewan

REGINA
WHITE CITY
BALGONIE
MCLEAN
QU'APPELLE
INDIAN HEAD
1
WOLSELEY
SUMMERBERRY
GRENFELL
BROADVIEW
WHITEWOOD
WAPELLA
MOOSOMIN
FLEMING
PRESENT TRANS CDA HWY
SASKATCHEWAN
MANITOBA

Map: Dawn Huck

AS IN WESTERN MANITOBA SECTION LINES DETERMINED THE ROUTE OF THE NO. 1 HIGHWAY UNTIL THE 1950S. EVENTUALLY NEWER CONSTRUCTION FOLLOWED THE EXAMPLE SET BY THE CPR.

SASKATCHEWAN PROVINCIAL FLOWER
WESTERN RED LILY

Mason Brock / www.en.wikipedia.org

The *Lilium philadelphicum* is also known as the wood lily, prairie lily, western red lily or Philadelphia lily. Its red or orange blossoms can be seen in meadows between June and early August, and year-round on Saskatchewan's provincial flag. Listed as endangered in many places in North America, by law wild lilies can not be picked, uprooted or destroyed.

Courtesy Of Fieldstone Campground

Above: Old Highway No. 1 West passes today's Fieldstone Campground, once owned by the government. Now privately run, it still boasts its beautifully constructed fieldstone-picnic shelter, among other features.

Below: Kaycie's Roadhouse. In the 1950s, the landmark building in Broadview sold handicrafts, not meals.

Clark Saunders

the railway crossing near the new hospital you can see all three cross-country routes: the road through town, the bypass that was built and paved by the early 1950s, and the newer bypass to the north.

In the early postwar years, westbound motorists would have headed north from here on gravel before turning west to Wapella. (It's a route that passes what is now the privately owned Fieldstone Campground but was formerly one of the four government-run campgrounds near the TCH spread across Saskatchewan.) Since the early 1950s, the highway has cut the corner, following the hypotenuse of the triangle, as it were. On the present route, just west of Moosomin, two sights greet the modern traveller that would have mystified our midcentury forebears. On the left is a large inland grain terminal of Parrish & Heimbecker Limited, while on the right stand the tall sentinels of a wind farm. A science-fiction aficionado of the 1950s might imagine that these latter structures with their enormous rotating blades were signs of an invasion by alien creatures from outer space.

Wapella and Whitewood are what they appear to be: small Saskatchewan towns that were connected by those right-angled unpaved roads until the early 1950s when a highway was constructed that paralleled the CPR. Both towns have been bypassed since then, although in both cases an exit into town leads onto a service road that was an earlier alignment of the highway. And again in both cases, a vestige of the old highway leads westward briefly before a barrier or break in the pavement announces that this is no longer a way out.

At Broadview, motorists have to leave the new four-lane highway if they want to pull up to the landmark now known as Kaycie's Roadhouse. It is located on the old route that for more than a half century brought travellers closer to the town. The original part of the building, located closest to the road, looks like a squat hexagonal lighthouse. It actually began its existence as a stylized teepee selling moccasins and other Aboriginal handicrafts. It was not until 1979 that it became a restaurant—the L.C. Corral. Since 2007, Kaycie has brought her own name and her own cooking and friendly hospitality to the establishment, feeding both locals and long-distance travellers.

The Sweet Dreams Motel, on the opposite corner of the old highway and Qu'Appelle Road, began life in 1962 as Edwards Motel.

The fresh-looking one-storey structure features a little fountain by the parking lot and in the lobby photos of each room to give sojourners an idea of what they are getting. Like Kaycie's, the Sweet Dreams expresses a soft spot for bikers with slogans like "Riders' Pride" and "Riders Rule".

Every town from the Manitoba boundary to Broadview lies to the south of the highway while every town from here to the outskirts of Regina is to the north. The reason for this is simple. Just west of Broadview the CPR mainline—which determined the location of towns—crosses under the highway from its left side to the right. From the modern overpass remains of the old highway can been seen to the north. (Older still is a route that takes vehicles *under* the rail line.) The next town worthy of the name—and the first to be found on the north side of the TCH—is Grenfell.

This is a good point to consider exploring the route as it was in the days before a paved highway bypassed these towns. Although the gravel road can be seen veering away on the right as travellers approach Grenfell, the best way to access it is by turning north on Highway 47 at the east edge of the town. From this highway a left turn made just before the track leads onto Front Avenue. Before following this road out into the countryside, it is worth taking time to appreciate this leafy town. The trees have had more than 60 years to mature since the middle of the last century and during the summer months, thoughtful citizens decorate the town centre with floral hanging baskets.

The gravel road leads west to the near-ghost town of Summerberry. When the National Film Board produced its tribute to the Trans-Canada Highway, *The Longest Road,* in 2003, Summerberry

Courtesy Of Town Of Broadview

Above: The railway underpass at Broadview is considered to be one of the town's important heritage features, allowing the CPR mainline and the old highway to coexist even before 1920.

Below: Grenfell's Main Street in an earlier day. Today, the grain elevator, as in so many prairie towns, is long gone.

Masalai / www.en.wikipedia.org

Saskatchewan in winter, sharing Manitoba's Central Time Zone. A summer version would colour Saskatchewan the bright green of Alberta's Mountain Time Zone.

IF IT'S THREE O'CLOCK IN WINNIPEG, WHAT TIME IS IT IN REGINA?

The answer to that question is not as straightforward as you might think. The question of Saskatchewan time is a convoluted one and over the years has presented a conundrum even to those who are not normally time zone challenged. You may feel confident about the fact that, if you are travelling west, somewhere between Brandon, Manitoba, and Medicine Hat, Alberta, you will gain an hour. But where? And when? And what does it all have to do with Broadview?

Well, timewise, Saskatchewan has a kind of split personality. Geographically it fits more comfortably with the Mountain Time Zone, but its eastern areas have always felt an affinity with the Central Time Zone. When standard time was introduced in 1912 each community was allowed to decide for itself which time zone it wished to adhere to. By 1925, the CPR was making the zone change at its divisional point of Broadview. And over the next few decades, motorists travelling east or west tended to adjust their watches at the same spot.

But with every community making

its own decision, things remained a bit chaotic. Some order was brought about in 1966 when the government decreed that the eastern part of the province would permanently be one hour ahead of Mountain Standard Time (that would be Central Standard Time, which is the same as Mountain Daylight Time). In the western part of the province, local governments could still follow either time zone. Almost all elected to do as the rest of the province was doing. Swift Current was the last holdout on the TCH. It finally gave in and agreed to match the rest of the province in 1972.

Today, nearly the entire province observes Central Standard Time all year round. That means that in the winter, if it's three o'clock in Winnipeg, it's also three o'clock in Regina. But in the summer, if it's three o'clock in Winnipeg, it's two o'clock in Regina. Of course, if it's two o'clock in Regina in the summer, it's also two o'clock in Calgary, since Central Standard Time (Regina) and Mountain Daylight Time (Calgary) are the same thing.

Well, I'm certainly glad we got that cleared up!

resident Shirley Gwilliam lamented what already felt like the death of this little place. It was the railway that determined that, in a world in which horse-drawn wagons transported grain to the nearest elevator, there should be a town every eight or 12 miles. It was the highway—and the vehicles that travelled it in a spirit of independence and ease—that decided that roughly every second town was redundant. At Summerberry, the grain elevator is no more. An abandoned but substantial two-storey school stands as a mute reminder of a time when the community teemed with life. It seems that most of the students who were educated in that building shook the dust of Summerberry from their feet and went on to seek their fortunes elsewhere.

Just west of Summerberry, the gravel road crosses the tracks before continuing on to Wolseley, a regional centre with an abundance of trees and a namesake motel. (The Wolseley Motel opened in 1960 and continues to boast 12 units, some with kitchenettes.) Those who laugh in the face of gravel may want to continue to Sintaluta and Indian Head on the old road, but discretion will lead others to follow signs leading to the TCH at either end of the town centre.

Approaching Indian Head on the modern highway motorists will find the federal government's experimental station to the north of the road near a campground. In operation since 1887 when it opened

Trees of many species from Indian Head's former Dominion Experimental Farm can be seen all across the prairies, where they create valuable shelter belts.

Peter St. John

Clark Saunders

Esso's Voyageur restaurants, marked by a "red hat" motif, were once common along Highway No. 1. Today, this one, at Indian Head, is a park shelter.

as the Dominion Experimental Farm, the station may attract fewer visitors today than it did in the middle of the last century. Now, as the Indian Head Experimental Farm, it focuses mostly on grain through its seed increase unit. But 60 years ago, when travellers had fewer attractions to claim their attention and the experimental station included farm animals in its areas of interest, there were more reasons for members of the general public to drop by and take a break from the miles and miles of Saskatchewan. For many itinerants one of those reasons was the opportunity to enjoy a picnic on the grounds.

Indian Head has commemorated its name in a large bust of an Aboriginal man in a headdress. It's a feature of the town that may elicit a variety of reactions. At any rate, a less controversial information booth stands nearby. Behind the booth, secured in cement, may be found a curious object resembling a large, red pointed hat. Travellers of a certain age may recognize it as the emblem of a chain of restaurants that used to be attached to Esso stations across the country. They were called "Voyageur" restaurants and catered to travellers who were ready to fill their gas tanks and their stomachs at a single stop. This particular red hat once adorned the roof of the restaurant attached to Don's Esso here in Indian Head.

Set about half way between the modern bypass and an earlier route closer to town, the Indian Head Motel with its bar and grill may pique curiosity about its age. The answer lies in its original name: Motel 61. It was a name that dated it in more ways than one.

A decision to rename it was only a matter of time. And what would the motel's first patrons have thought if someone had told them that a half century later a sitcom called *Little Mosque on the Prairie* would be filmed in Indian Head? Undoubtedly they would have had questions to ask—but where to begin?

Sixteen kilometers farther west, the village of Qu'Appelle can be discerned off to the north. Highway No. 1 has not gone through it since the 1950s. But Highway 35 does. In fact, it beckons those with a little time to spare to spend some of it in the surprising and beautiful Qu'Appelle Valley that lies 20 kilometres northward.

Indian Head was the setting for the CBC sitcom *Little Mosque on the Prairie*, filmed between 2007 and 2012.

Until the mid-'50s, a zigzagging gravel highway crossed the next village—McLean—from north to south before continuing its westward route on pavement to Regina. At the time, this was the first pavement a motorist would have encountered since entering the province from the east.

There isn't much to see in McLean. But campers of an earlier time will recall the provincial government campground that lay south of the highway and just west of town. The sad news is that the government closed it many years ago, and tourists camp there no more.

The route from here into Regina has been modified repeatedly over the years. Until the early 1950s, the road led straight west from Balgonie, passed Pilot Butte and entered the city at its north end. (After being superseded by a more southerly alignment, this road disappeared from highway maps until it was revived in more recent times as Highway 46; it can be accessed from the TCH at Balgonie.) By 1955, a new highway had been built angling southwest at Balgonie before following a direct westward route straight into the heart of the city. Then on August 21, 1957, Premier T.C. Douglas cut the ribbon that both opened the Regina bypass and marked the completion of the paving of Saskatchewan's stretch of the Trans-Canada Highway.

From that moment on, traffic with no need to stop in Regina has used the bypass. By 1965, the few miles from Balgonie to Regina had become the first section of the highway in Saskatchewan to be twinned. In fits and starts, the work continued until, by the early years of the 21st century, the TCH had finally become a divided highway across the entire province.

The last town before the highway reaches the capital is the commuter community of White City. There are a number of clues to suggest its Johnny-come-lately status: its location was not determined by the railway, which does not pass through or near it. It does

Tommy Douglas (shown here in 1945) was Saskatchewan premier in 1957 when paving the province's portion of the TCH was completed.

Lieut. G. Barry Gilroy / www.en.wikipedia.org

SK Archives Photo R-B5902

A blizzard in southern Saskatchewan in 1947 piled enormous snowdrifts along the Trans-Canada Highway.

not appear on provincial roadmaps until the 1960s. And it was not even designated a hamlet until 1958.

Regina has changed a lot since that day in 1957 when Tommy Douglas opened the bypass. The Queen City had a population of about 100,000 in those days; it is almost twice that size today. However, although it retains the distinction of being the provincial capital, by 1980 Saskatoon had displaced it as the province's largest city and continues to outstrip Regina in growth.

Sitting as it does on a level plain, Regina's skyline can be seen from a long way off. But although a number of taller buildings were to pop up in the 1960s, in 1957, motorists approaching the city from a distance would make out only the Hotel Saskatchewan and the dome of the provincial legislature etched against the prairie sky.

Until the day the bypass opened, motorists crossing the province had to cross the city as well. What is now the city route continues straight west on Victoria Avenue. Like Highway 1A through Brandon (another Victoria Avenue) this is for the most part a gracious residential street with a central boulevard. In the centre of the city, Victoria meets her consort, Albert, and the route travels south for 5½ kilometres until it encounters the bypass again.

Weary travellers are still welcomed at the east end of the city by a wide choice of accommodations. Today, most of the hotels and motels belong to chains, although the Sunrise Motel just inside the bypass has the look of one of the old independents. Gone, however, is a short-lived motel that consisted of an assortment of trailers of various sizes. Imagine the excitement experienced by children of the 1950s who succeeded in persuading their parents to let the family spend a night in an actual trailer!

In the early postwar decades, families overnighting in Regina and in search of diversion had a number of choices available to them. One was paying a visit to the RCMP Academy, Depot Division, commonly known simply as "the Depot". It is still there. It is reached by turning right from Victoria Avenue onto Albert Street and then going west on Dewdney Avenue and continuing past the spacious grounds of Government House. Today, the site is dominated by a state-of-the-art tourist-magnet, the RCMP Heritage Centre, which was opened in 2007. But to the south of this impressive glass, metal and stone structure, visitors can still find reminders of the things that drew tourists of past generations to this part of the city.

Dating back to the days of the North West Mounted Police, the oldest existing building in Regina began life as a guardhouse in 1885, the year that the training of NWMP cadets began on this site—and the year Louis Riel was hanged on a spot nearby. Ten years later, the building was converted for use as a chapel, a function it continues to perform to this day. Beginning in 1933, visitors were also able to explore a modest museum that was housed in a series of locations at the Depot until, after the museum's closure in 2006, its collections found their way into the new Heritage Centre. The Drill Hall, dating from 1929, can still be seen, as can the old cemetery. And visitors of today, like of those of the last century, may be lucky enough to time their visit to coincide with one of the force's ceremonies held on the parade ground. They will be less likely to see horses, however. Horsemanship was dropped from standard cadet training in 1966.

Other things have changed, too. Today's cadets are on average

RCMP cadets march outside the RCMP Academy in Regina. The "Depot", as the academy is called, has been training cadets since 1885.

Brian Dell / www.en.wikipedia.org

Lorraine Brecht / www.en.wikipedia.org

Above: Wascana Centre's Trafalgar Fountain, installed in 1963, is one of a pair that played in Trafalgar Square, London, from 1845 to 1939.

Below: The dam of Albert Memorial Bridge on Wascana Creek created the Wascana Lake reservoir, the centrepiece of the park.

about 10 years older than their counterparts in the 1950s and '60s. They are generally more highly educated and more ethnically diverse and the proportion of women has increased. Though surrounded at times by controversy and calls for reform, the force's links with the past remain strong and are nowhere more evident than in Regina.

The Depot lies to the west of Regina's city centre. To the south, Wascana Park has been a draw for locals and tourists alike for more than a century. One of the largest urban parks in Canada, this green space wraps itself around Wascana Lake, formed by the damming of Wascana Creek. With all those Wascanas, you might wonder why the name was not given to the city. Well, in a way it was. Wascana (or Oscana) is a Cree word meaning "pile of bones," and that, in fact, was Regina's original name. "Pile of Bones" may not run trippingly off the tongue, but "Wascana" sounds downright poetic. Some might think that Queen Victoria would have been satisfied to have just one Canadian provincial capital named after her and would not mind this one reverting to its Aboriginal name.

Since its completion in 1912, the provincial legislative building has impressed visitors to the park. Like the domed legislatures of the

Scotwood72 / www.en.wikipedia.org

Canstockphoto/CSP - 5837614

other western provinces, Saskatchewan's seat of government speaks of a grandeur and a confidence that are hard to credit when one considers that the province was in its infancy when this structure rose on the nearly treeless plain. No doubt it would have made a more modest impression if it had been faced with brick as was originally planned. At the last minute, it was decided to face it with Tyndall stone quarried from the same town in Manitoba that provided the limestone to give a sense of dignity to so many other public buildings in Canada.

A half century after Saskatchewan became a province, the provincial museum found a permanent home in the northwest corner of the park. Known at the time as the Saskatchewan Museum of Natural History, it was opened on May 16, 1955 by Canada's first home-

Saskatchewan's Legislative Building. Built in the Beaux-Arts style popular in the early 20th century, it was constructed between 1908 and 1912.

Clark Saunders

The Royal Saskatchewan Museum stands where a grand railway hotel was partially built before the First World War, but never completed.

grown governor general, Vincent Massey. The Queen visited in 1959, but it was not until 34 years later that a royal designation was granted to the museum. Today it is the Royal Saskatchewan Museum.

From the day it opened, those who have enjoyed the exhibits displayed in this clean-lined, quietly elegant midcentury structure have not been limited to the citizens of Regina or Saskatchewan. Families travelling across the country and finding themselves with an hour or two to spare have been educated and entertained by the dioramas that seemed the latest thing in museum displays when the building first opened. Since the '50s, the museum's managers have worked at keeping pace with trends toward hands-on and interactive exhibits. Today, its features may not seem exceptional in the world of modern museums, but to baby boomer kids and their parents a half century ago its approach seemed strikingly avant-garde.

The odd angle at which the building sits in relation to the neighbouring streets might seem the result of an architect's whim or a designer's sense of style. But it is neither. The fact is that the museum sits on the foundation of a hotel that never was.

Before the First World War the Grand Trunk Pacific Railway planned to build an imposing hotel on the site. It would have reflected the French chateau style of other Canadian railway hotels, but with a Scottish baronial twist. Alas, labour and material shortages and the eventual bankruptcy of the railway ensured that the structure never amounted to anything more than a five-storey eyesore composed of skeletal steel girders. Eventually these were dismantled. But two subterranean storeys of reinforced concrete were less easily disposed of. When the time came to build a new museum the problem was used to advantage. The hotel's intended basement became the foundation of the Museum of Natural History.

Opposite: Canstockphoto/CSP - 7402149

4

from
REGINA
~ to the ALBERTA
BORDER

HARVESTING SCENES IN SASKATCHEWAN

Early Harvesting Poster

A fter running south from downtown Regina on Albert Street, the city route rejoins the bypass south of the city. From here the Trans-Canada Highway runs straight west to Moose Jaw. Although pavement was added in the 1940s and the road became a four-lane affair in 1968, the route remains essentially what it has been since drivers first took a notion to travel between Regina and Moose Jaw.

A midcentury motorist driving this stretch of highway and passing the village of Belle Plaine could have gazed northward and seen nothing but waving fields of grain. Not so today. One of Saskatchewan's 10 potash mines dominates the horizon as it has since it opened in 1964.

In the middle of the 20th century, the subject of potash had yet to register on Saskatchewan's consciousness. Although the crop nutrient was discovered in 1942 when prospectors looking for oil stumbled upon it, 20 years would elapse before production would begin at Esterhazy. Since then the industry has experienced ups and downs: flooded mines that required new technology to become viable, glutted markets, periods of greater provincial government involvement followed by periods of privatization. Through it all Saskatchewan emerged as the world's largest producer of potash. Yet, travellers passing Belle Plaine a decade before the mine opened might never have heard the word. To them the most notable thing about the village might have been the fact that this was where the highway crossed the railway tracks.

In fact, the little village of Belle Plaine is where the only real change to this stretch of the route has been made. Just west of town

Above and opposite: From the earliest settlement period to midcentury and beyond, travellers east of Regina would have been greeted by grain and grass.

is the spot where the railway line, running very nearly parallel to the highway, intersects with it on its mostly westward but ever so slightly southward way from Regina to Moose Jaw. For years the highway made a slight jog so that it could cross the railway at something like a right angle. But a busy railway crossing a busy highway was a situation that created problems. Aside from the inherent dangers, road traffic was frequently held up for minutes at a time. By the 1960s, inconvenienced motorists could rejoice in the completion of an overpass. The overpass may be a boon to travellers in a hurry, but it can be icy in winter and the wind can blow fiercely at any time of year. In fact, this spot has become notorious for its ability to flip a semitrailer off its wheels. The inconvenience of waiting for a train to pass may seem minor when compared with the inconvenience of waiting for an injured semi to be hauled off the highway—not to mention the terror of watching it lose its balance before your very eyes.

After they have negotiated the overpass, seasoned westbound travellers know the signs that indicate Moose Jaw is not far off. A modest valley opens up on the right while the highway from Weyburn merges from the left. Shortly after this intersection a modern motel—currently a Thriftlodge—appears, also on the left. But hiding behind the newer building is the original motel that for decades before the operation expanded was offering roadside accommodation

A sight that was not uncommon on the old highways across the prairies: unbarricaded railway crossings.

Canstockphoto/CSP - 0765572

western saskatchewan

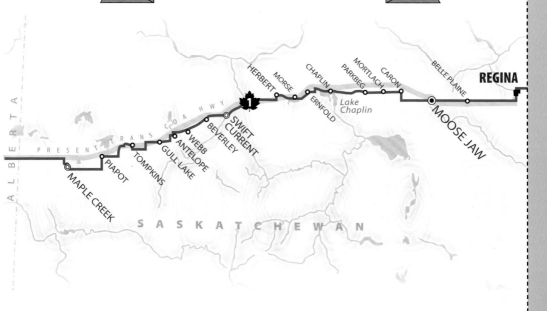

Map: Dawn Huck

ACROSS THE PRAIRIES THE OLD HIGHWAY WENT THROUGH MANY TOWNS THAT WERE LATER BYPASSED. IN THE EARLY 1950S ENGINEERS WHO REFUSED TO BE INTIMIDATED BY SECTION LINES MANAGED TO ELIMINATE MORE THAN 30 KILOMETRES OF ROAD BETWEEN SWIFT CURRENT AND THE ALBERTA BOUNDARY.

SASKATCHEWAN PROVINCIAL TREE

WHITE BIRCH

Canstockphoto/CSP - 8376265

Adopted as the province's tree in 1988, *Betula papyrifera* is easily recognized by its white, papery bark. Long used across North America to build canoes, baskets and utensils, the bark is also a suitable substitute for paper. Strong and flexible, the wood was used to make bows and arrows, spears, snowshoes and sleds and today is often used for making furniture.

Canstockphoto/CSP - 4520440

Above: Moose Jaw City Hall today. Before 1965, it was a combination post office RCMP station, and government office.

Below: St. Andrew's United Church, Moose Jaw.

Clark Saunders

to motorists who wanted to avoid adding time to their journey by entering the city.

Since the late 1950s, through traffic has been able to avoid Moose Jaw by taking the bypass around the north edge of town. But Moose Jaw has a lot to offer those who will take the exit onto "No. 1 Alternate" (a.k.a. the grandly titled Manitoba Expressway) and then split off onto Athabasca Street East. Today, this older city route still passes the Dreamland Motel, a relic of an earlier age. (Judging from the number of vintage motels along the way with similar names, the implied promise of pleasant dreams seems to have been a big sell in those days.) On the same street and across from a small park near the heart of the city stands an imposing neo-Gothic church dating from the years before the First World War. St. Andrew's United Church, called by some "the cathedral of the prairies", was largely destroyed by fire in 1963. Restored to its former glory, it is one of a number of buildings in Moose Jaw that speak of the confidence its early citizens had in the future of this railway town. Another example is the former train station itself, built in the early 1920s. With its clock tower—faced in (you guessed it) Tyndall stone looking up Main Street, the station still defines the place.

Two of Moose Jaw's present attractions date back a long way, but when tourists came to town in the first decades after the Second World War their potential was still unrealized. In fact, if anyone had suggested in those days that Moose Jaw would become a spa town, most people would have laughed at the idea. Geothermal water

Courtesy Of The Tunnels Of Moose Jaw

might have been located under the city as far back as 1910, but it would not be until 1980 that practical use could be made of it. Since then, Moose Jaw has become a destination for those who want to be soothed and pampered while taking the waters.

The Tunnels of Moose Jaw are another attraction that was not available to tourists of the mid-20th century. Oh, the tunnels were there, all right. They date back to the days when steam was the method of heating downtown buildings. And whether they knew it or not, midcentury pedestrians in the downtown area were walking above a network of tunnels that had already provided shelter for Chinese immigrants and figured in the illicit liquor trade of the years between the wars. But it would be many years before the local tourism industry would capitalize on these associations and on the tunnels' alleged ties to Al Capone and his minions.

Dating back to those interwar years and with an unbroken history right up to the present is the River Park Campground. Begun by the city as an "auto tourist camp" in 1927, this campground claims to be one of the oldest continuously operating campgrounds in North America. It is reached by taking Highway 2 south from the east end of downtown, crossing the Moose Jaw River and exiting on to River Drive. Nestled in a bend in the river's Wakamow Valley, the campground is on the right just after the drive crosses another bridge.

Did Al Capone frequent Moose Jaw's nether regions? The Tunnels of Moose Jaw tourist attraction says so. But it would have been news to midcentury travellers.

Below: A vintage building at River Park Campground.

Clark Saunders

Built on the site of an old brick-making plant, River Park Campground opened in a time when modern RVs and trailers were unknown. Instead it provided a row of cabins. During a housing shortage after the Second World War these cabins were pressed into service to accommodate returning servicemen. Eventually most of the buildings were removed, but a couple of them, including one known as "the cook shack", remain. Otherwise the postwar years have seen a steady transition to the kind of campground most of us recognize. The city still owns the land and the current manager holds a life lease on it.

Whether they stayed in a campground or a motel, travellers heading west from Moose Jaw prior to the building of the bypass would have taken Caribou Street west from Main. It is a route worth taking today. As Municipal Road 735 it passes through first residential and then industrial areas before emerging into the countryside and heading toward an escarpment. It begins a journey into western Saskatchewan that sees steadily fewer farms and more ranches while flat terrain with at least a modicum of trees gives way to rolling and largely treeless grassland.

Dramatic prairie skies near Caron, Saskatchewan.

At a spot directly south of Caron, this mostly unpaved old route turns north on what is now municipal road 643. At the village the old highway turns west again. The modern driver may have seen

Peter St. John

Brian Wolitski / bmwphotos.smugmug.com

enough of gravel roads by now, however, and will be content to continue north a couple of kilometres to the modern highway.

Five kilometres east of Caron drivers who chose the bypass route around Moose Jaw will have passed a town that was not found on highway maps until about 1960. Caronport had a previous existence as RCAF Station Caron (known locally as Caron Airport). After the Second World War it was deemed redundant. It happened that Briercrest Bible College was outgrowing its original home in the town that provided its name. Its leaders saw an opportunity to buy some surplus buildings and a new site on which to expand. Most of the original buildings are gone now, but the college campus and the town of Caronport are virtually one and the same. From the modern highway you can't miss Caronport, but it is easy to drive past Caron, the village it is named for, without noticing it south of the highway, nestled in a shallow valley.

Burrowing owls were a relatively common prairie sight for midcentury travellers. Today, however, the little ground-dwelling owls are endangered in Canada. Moose Jaw's Burrowing Owl Interpretive Centre works to promote their conservation.

Saskatchewan is full of surprises. One is the Besant Campground located south of the TCH between Caron and Mortlach. Who would expect to find a wooded area complete with a spring-fed pond in the midst of the prairie?

Recreational Vehicles

WITH EVERYTHING FROM TENTS to canvas-top tent trailers and hard-top pop-up trailers, from campervans and "fifth wheels" to top-of-the-line silver aluminum Airstream travel trailers, in the postwar years many North American highway travellers opted to take their accommodations with them. Their travel day ended not in a motel, but in a campground. In the boom times after the war, when road trip vacations became more popular, these sojourners were part of an expansion in the field of what we now call "recreational vehicles"—an expansion that has continued into the 21st century.

For those who had places to go and people to see, one night per campground was the norm. The more modest the RV, the more labour intensive the travelling experience would be. Those who travelled with the simplest gear would be putting up a tent at the end of the day and taking it down in the morning and, more likely than not, cooking their meals on a Coleman stove. They usually took longer to get away in the morning and were sometimes left to envy the vehicles that came with no assembly required.

The amenities in the campgrounds varied greatly as well. In the early days electricity might not be available. Plumbing could range from the luxury of hot and cold running water to something much more primitive. (When she was a girl, staying with her family at a campsite on the Trans-Canada, a woman of my acquaintance lost her way while returning to home base from a nocturnal visit to the outhouse; her cries of "Dad!" were met with responses from a chorus of sleepy masculine voices.)

As to the management of these campgrounds, some were operated by a local authority, some were provincial facilities, and some were privately owned. Some were stand-alone operations, while others were part of a chain. From its beginnings in Billings, Montana, in 1962, the Kampgrounds of America (KOA) franchise spread across the United States and into Canada and set a fairly high standard in the quality of its amenities. The Airstreamers went them one better. Not only did they get together at their own rallies, south of the border they even built some of their own trailer parks where there was no need to associate with riff-raff and they could hobnob exclusively with their own kind.

In a frenzy of late-20th century privatization, both the Manitoba and Saskatchewan governments took steps toward getting out of the camping business. Manitoba sold off all of its campgrounds except some that were located in provincial parks. Along the TCH Saskatchewan eventually found buyers for campgrounds located near three of the four "M"s—Moosomin, Mortlach and Maple Creek—but the one at McLean remains closed.

Camping continues to be the preferred way to go for many who hit the road. And even those who stay in motels still appreciate the occasional picnic at some roadside stop. Although a picnic area on the prairies in the 1950s could be treeless and unwelcoming, in the mountains it was likely to come complete with babbling brook and cedar- or pine-scented air. In a spot like that, tourists were inclined to linger long enough to feel refreshed before tackling the rest of the day.

Another surprise is Mortlach itself. Before it was bypassed in the late 1950s, Mortlach sat right on the highway as it ran directly west from Caron. The town centre is located two blocks south of this old route. As one might expect, downtown Mortlach includes a number of buildings that were far from new when midcentury travellers passed through town.

But Mortlach has spiffied itself up and its businesses appear quaint rather than dowdy. An improbable town that can muster 250 inhabitants on a good day, it even has a New Age air about it. Gift shops market healing crystals and fossils as well as arts and crafts and antiques. Farmers gathered around a table in front of the Country Garden Teahouse and Café on a summer morning could well be drinking lattes—something beyond the ken of their fathers and grandfathers a half century ago.

Those who make the worthwhile detour into Mortlach would be well advised to return to the modern highway before proceeding westward rather than following the old alignment directly west from the town. The reason: four miles (or about seven kilometres) west of Mortlach the old highway lines up with the eastbound lanes of the divided highway. The sight of traffic coming toward you at speeds in excess of 110 kilometres per hour is something no one really wants to see. Never mind that this oncoming traffic is on a route that will ensure that they veer to their left before they reach you.

Courtesy of the village of Mortlach.

Mortlach, Saskatchewan, is an oasis of charm.

For several kilometres from this point the eastbound and westbound lanes of the divided highway run about a kilometre apart from each other—divided indeed. Until the early 1950s, the highway followed what are now the eastbound lanes as far as Parkbeg where it made a jog to the north and proceeded west on what are now the westbound lanes. When that jog was eliminated most of the other 90-degree turns between Parkbeg and Swift Current were smoothed out as well.

The bypass around the south side of Chaplin dates from just a few years later. The older highway can be most easily accessed by means of a right turn onto Highway 19. The old road is the one that runs through town on the south side of the tracks.

Both old and new routes will bring motorists within sight of what look like piles of snow. This is actually sodium sulphate drawn from Lake Chaplin, the second largest saline body of water in Canada. The provincial government opened a plant to process the stuff in 1948. Until then, farmers in the area had struggled with poor land.

Both Images: Peter St. John

The Nature Centre near the Village of Chaplin offers useful information about the ecology of Lake Chaplin (above), the second-largest saline body of fresh water in Canada. For summer travellers then and now, the sodium-sulphate landscape around the lake looks snowy, not salty.

(Salty water makes for salty soil.) But although Chaplin did not exactly become a boomtown, the local economy took a marked turn for the better. Passers-by have been intrigued by the fake snow ever since.

The lake can even take credit for such tourism as Chaplin enjoys. Birdwatchers spot the sanderlings and piping plovers and about 30 other species of shorebirds who stop to rest, breed and chow down on a meal of brine shrimp before migrating onward. That's to say, the birds migrate onwards; eventually the birdwatchers move on as well.

Explorers of the old route may want to follow it west from the centre of town and out beyond the Saskatchewan Minerals plant. But before long this gravel road simply parallels the new highway on its north side from which it can easily be seen.

Travellers on either road might enjoy a brief stop in Uren. A sign on the lawn of one of its few properties lists its population as eight. In fact, it is so small that for decades motorists have missed it entirely. Surely ours was not the only family to study the map and ask, "Have we passed Uren yet?" It might have been an innocent question the first time it was asked. But it was sure to be trotted out again every time our travels took us past this spot. (No doubt we would have felt deflated if we had known that local pronunciation comes closer to "earn" than to "yearn.")

By the late 1950s, Uren had been bypassed. From this point the modern westbound and eastbound lanes of the four-lane actually wander off at a great distance from one another before coming together again near Ernfold, a spot that claims to be the only village on the entire TCH route to be located between its eastbound and westbound lanes.

At Morse, motorists have always had to skirt the northern edge of Reed Lake (another salty pond popular with bird traffic), which lies to the south. In an earlier time, though, they followed what is now Railway Avenue South, which gave them at least a passing acquaintance with the town; that is more than the present route does.

Clark Saunders

Tiny Uren, Saskatch-ewan, like many small prairie communities, once had a one-room schoolhouse. All that remains of Uren's School District 549 is this sign.

The last jog to be eliminated from the highway between Moose Jaw and Swift Current came just west of Herbert. It appears on highway maps as late as 1965. Until a few years before that, the route into Swift Current had taken the direct approach—direct into the heart of town, that is, on Chaplin Street. The location of a motel at 150 21st Avenue Southeast is a reminder that the old city route passed nearby. Having begun life as a motel, what is now the Silver Saddle became for a time a residence for a Bible college before reverting to its original identity, but under a new name. In the years when the old highway came right through the city, travellers were more likely than they are today to patronize downtown eateries like the Modern Family Restaurant. The place has been around since Swift Current's early days and, when it was in the hands of Chinese-Canadian owners, included Chinese items on the menu. Midcentury travellers would have encountered not only a different menu, but a different ambience as well; today's fresh new booths, wall-to-wall carpets and dim lighting create an atmosphere that patrons from earlier generations would hardly recognize. In fact, they might have asked someone to turn on the lights.

Since the '50s, cross-country travellers have tended not to drive into Swift Current's city centre. That was when a new route was built, coming in from the east on a west-by-south-westerly trajectory that passes along the north edge of town. The new route created a "strip" that remains the primary locale of accommodations and eating places for the travelling public. Today, the Days Inn stands on the spot once occupied by an early contender, the Horseshoe Lodge Motel. A welcome oasis in this sparsely settled landscape, the Horseshoe featured a restaurant across the front of the building and rooms arranged in a continuous horseshoe to the rear with a swimming pool in the courtyard in the middle.

Clark Saunders

The welcoming sign of Swift Current's Safari Inn, which opened in 1964, is a tribute to the popular design and colours of the mid-20th century.

Saskatchewan Archives

Paving the Trans-Canada Highway west of Swift Current in 1954.

The Horseshoe is gone now. It disappeared in the mid-'90s. But other independents continue to ply their trade among the newer chains. Some, like the Safari Inn, which opened in 1964, have retained their period look without losing their freshness. The Safari's turquoise-and-white colour scheme is right out of the '50s, and its tall period-piece sign is topped with three stylized spears emblematic of its name. Others dating from the same period include the Caravel, the Rainbow and the City Centre (all on the strip) and, a kilometre or two farther west on the modern highway and with a restaurant included, the K Motel.

It was in 1951 that engineers got down to the business of planning a route that would eliminate more than 30 kilometres of highway between Swift Current and the Alberta boundary. Until then, the road west from Swift Current had done a little jog—first west, then south—before making for Beverley on an alignment that ran along the south side of the railway. A new stretch of highway was built that stayed north of the tracks. From Beverley to Webb the engineers left the route much as they found it, but from Webb westward there were several twists and turns to be ironed out as it passed Antelope—a hamlet that is no longer on the map (though if you are lucky you may see one of the pronghorns for which it was named)—and continued on to Gull Lake.

Motorists of the 1950s who had noticed signs of recent oil and gas discoveries as they passed Virden, Manitoba, would see similar evidence as they drove by Gull Lake. The pumps are still at work in the vicinity. At the beginning of the '50s, drivers would have continued straight west on unpaved road to a point north of Carmichael and then turned straight south to that town. By the middle of the decade, drivers on a new highway (then itself only a gravel road) would see this road crossing their path at an angle just west of Gull Lake. In fact, the former route can still be seen today.

The changes of the early '50s sidelined Carmichael as the new alignment ran more directly to Tomkins and Sidewood. The provincial highway map of 1955 still includes an old route from Sidewood to Piapot (first south, then west) but also shows the new highway as a more direct option, though neither road was paved. Again at Piapot, both the old and new highways are shown. As at Sidewood, the

Brian Wolitski / bmwphotos.smugmug.com

old road runs first south, then west. In 1955, a new route—the one modern travellers use—was being completed that would miss Maple Creek by 11 kilometres. Transcontinental travellers passing so far to the north would no longer stop in at Maple Creek unless they had a good reason to go there.

The old route from Piapot to Maple Creek is still worth exploring though. Today, it is traced by taking Municipal Road 614 south (paved), then turning onto Municipal Road 724 west (mostly gravel). The journey crosses rangeland and fields dotted with hay bales. After its turn westward it crosses a little valley and leads on to hilly high country that affords spacious views in all directions. Along the way the road passes three old bridges, two of them of the "rainbow arch" variety and all of them indicating the location of an older road of which no other sign remains.

Eventually Municipal Road 724 descends from the heights. About three kilometres before reaching Maple Creek, gravel gives way to pavement. The approach to the town gives a good idea of what it must have been like 60 years ago to travel across the lonely plains and behold at last the welcome sight of civilization.

Like many prairie towns Maple Creek's businesses include a Chinese restaurant. In fact, during the Second World War when soldiers were stationed here prior to being sent overseas, some of them used to patronize it. My father was one of them. It was called the BC Café. It is still there at 122 Jasper Street. At least two generations of the Wong family served Chinese and Canadian dishes

It was pronghorn like these, often colloquially and erroneously called "antelope" in the past, that inspired the naming of a now-faded village in the region.

During much of the 20th century, travellers would have been lucky to see these ancient and elegant creatures. Now, thanks to conservation programs across North America, motorists are much more likely to spot them.

Clark Saunders

The BC Café in Maple Creek, Saskatchewan. Once upon a time, a steak dinner there cost just 50 cents. Inflation has intruded since.

at the café before they sold it a few years ago to Lucy and Alan Lee.

My father used to talk about the great steak dinners he could get for 50 cents at the BC Café. By the time he took his family there for dinner on a road trip to the West Coast nearly 20 years later, the price had risen to $1.50. But the steak still made an impression with its sizzle. Served on heated metal platters, it arrived piping hot.

For today's motorist, the way back to the Trans-Canada Highway is via Highway 21. But before the construction of the new section of TCH north of Maple Creek, the way forward led from the northwest corner of the town. Highway 21 comes up from the Cypress Hills, runs along the west side of town, and makes a sharp-angled turn at this corner to run east as Pacific Avenue, parallel to the railway tracks. But a road continues north from this sharp intersection. It is Range Road 3264 and it is the old highway. It runs north, then west and north again, crossing a narrow truss bridge on its way to intersect with the modern Trans-Canada a few kilometres west of the TCH's crossing with Highway 21.

Just east of the intersection of Range Road 3264 and the TCH is the Eagle Valley Park Campground, the most westerly of the campgrounds formerly operated by the Province of Saskatchewan. Situated in a valley on the south side of the highway, the campground was pretty barren and treeless a couple of generations ago. Today, campers will find trees providing shade and shelter from the merciless Saskatchewan summer sun. But the campground's recent history has been checkered. After sitting idle for a decade, it reopened in 2002 only to fall victim to the flooding of the TCH in 2010. The place is nothing if not resilient. Just as there was no question that the highway would be repaired, the campground carries on and continues to welcome travellers.

But another province is almost in view. After all the route changes that shortened the highway east of Maple Creek in the 1950s, the route of the Trans-Canada from the campground to the Alberta boundary has changed little since the Second World War.

Opposite: Peter St. John

from the
ALBERTA
BORDER
~ to CALGARY

The coulees and rolling grasslands of southwestern Saskatchewan provide travellers with a foretaste of what awaits them in southern Alberta. But the approach to the next province actually involves a descent from the hills and offers a view of Alberta's first town, Walsh, sitting in the distance on the plain. Mind you, Walsh is not quite so easy to spot since it lost its grain elevator. But the tourist information centre is still there. It comes into view soon after you pass the boundary marker and notice a change in the pavement. The centre is certainly worthy of a stop. Walsh has little else to offer the traveller, although the curious might want to drive into the village and find Reinhart Street. It is a short section of an earlier alignment of the Trans-Canada Highway.

Southeastern Alberta remains the land of prairie sagebrush and juniper, prickly pear cactus and the provincial emblem, the wild rose. Something else that has not changed over the years in this part of the country is the velocity with which the wind can come sweeping down the plain. It is the same wind that comes rushing through the Crowsnest Pass and gives Lethbridge the reputation of being a windy city. It is the same wind that for decades has been able to exhaust motorists as they have clung to the steering wheel and considered ending the day early.

Another thing that shows few signs of change is the 50-kilometre route from Walsh to Medicine Hat. Some of the bends in the road may have been smoothed out, but the path it follows is essentially the same as it was at the end of the Second World War. The few towns along the way have changed, though. If Irvine looks smaller than it did years ago, it is because some residents pulled up stakes in the wake of the devastation caused by the same flooding that damaged the highway and the Eagle Valley Park Campground in Western Saskatchewan in 2010.

OPPOSITE: The dry valley slopes of the South Saskatchewan River at Medicine Hat.

Unlike Swift Current, which has grown only slightly since the early postwar years, Medicine Hat's population has tripled (to more than 60,000) since 1955. Its suburbs have spread south and west of the Trans-Canada bypass that opened that year. Most of the city's vintage motels are clustered around the interchange between Highways 1 and 3. On the service road along the southwest side of the TCH near that junction, the Ranchmen's cartoon cowboy still grins from his lofty, eye-catching sign, while next door it seems that the original owners of the Satellite turned for inspiration to the space race of the late '50s when it came to naming their motel.

There was an earlier time, of course, when the highway went through the city centre. To get a sense of this, motorists may try taking the exit at Dunmore Road as they come in from the east. Almost immediately Dunmore Road bends northwestward. From this point it follows the path of the old highway. The alignment leads onward via Kingsway and South Railway Street to the heart of town. Here the pale brick of Medicine Hat's oldest buildings serve as a reminder of the things that brought the town into existence in the first place.

In the 1880s, the town's pioneers discovered that clay and natural gas were a winning combination. The clay was easy to see—and to mine. It was right there in the rugged cliffs around the town. The discovery of natural gas in the area provided a cheap source of energy. (It also prompted Rudyard Kipling, who stopped by for a visit in 1907, to famously describe the area as having "all hell for a basement." Local tourism has been trading on that line ever since.) Medicine Hat's most conspicuous resources entered a symbiotic relationship that resulted in the production of pottery and bricks that ended up all over the country. (When I was a boy my mother had an enormous clay mixing-bowl that came from Medicine Hat.) One of the larger factories was Medalta Potteries. It closed in 1954, but today visitors can tour its virtually untouched facilities to view some of its products and see how they were made. The old plant is located at 713 Medalta Avenue SE in the Historic Clay District east of the tracks.

It was local clay that was used for making the bricks that provided building material for Medicine Hat's downtown. And today, when half the towns in Western Canada seem to have murals painted on the walls of some of their commercial buildings, Medicine Hat is unique in displaying murals created out of bricks by local artist,

Working with natural clay from the valley near Medicine Hat, Medalta Potteries, now a national historic site, was part of Western Canada's earliest industry. Today, it is both an interpretive museum and a working enterprise, producing heritage pottery that is sold in its gift shop.

Cortesy of www.virtualmuseum.ca

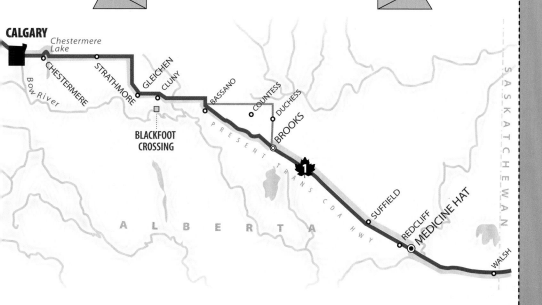

CALGARY
Chestermere Lake
Bow River
CHESTERMERE
STRATHMORE
GLEICHEN
CLUNY
BLACKFOOT CROSSING
BASSANO
COUNTESS
DUCHESS
BROOKS
PRESENT TRANS CDA HWY
ALBERTA
SUFFIELD
REDCLIFF
MEDICINE HAT
WALSH
SASKATCHEWAN

Map: Dawn Huck

MUCH OF THE MODERN ROUTE PARALLELS THE OLD HIGHWAY IN EASTERN ALBERTA, ALTHOUGH IN SOME PLACES RIGHT ANGLES WERE REPLACED BY MORE DIRECT DIAGONAL ALIGNMENTS. AMONG THE MOST SIGNIFICANT CHANGES MADE IN THE EARLY 1950S WAS ONE THAT ELIMINATED THE LONG DRIVE NORTH FROM BROOKS TO A POINT BEYOND DUCHESS BEFORE IT TURN WEST TOWARD BASSANO.

ALBERTA PROVINCIAL FLOWER

WILD ROSE

Alberta adopted the wild rose, *Rosa Acicularis,* as its official flower in 1930, following a suggestion by the editor of an Edmonton newspaper. The Women's Institute took up the suggestion, passed it on to the Department of Education, and the province's schoolchildren made the final choice. Growing throughout the Northern Hemisphere's northern regions, it is also known as the prickly wild rose, the bristly rose and the Arctic rose. Its seeds or hips, which are full of vitamin C, were gathered in huge numbers during the Second World War as a replacement for oranges.

QUESTION: What do Kirkella, Manitoba, Fleming, Saskatchewan, and Walsh, Alberta have in common (besides being the first community you encounter after crossing a provincial boundary on the Trans-Canada Highway)?

ANSWER: They all used to have one grain elevator, or more. Today they have none.

Grain elevators once stood sentinel in almost every prairie town, but innovations in grain transportation have made them redundant.

Some called them "prairie giants". Others, alluding to the medieval churches that dominate European towns, referred to them as "the cathedrals of the plains". The location of a town was easy to spot because of the grain elevators that rose skyward beside the railway tracks. Many could be seen for miles around. And there was no need to search for a town's name on a highway sign. It was emblazoned in much larger letters on the side of the elevator.

But the number of traditional, wood-cribbed elevators on the prairies has declined dramatically since the middle of the last century. The numbers for Saskatchewan illustrate the point. In 1950, there were 3,035 primary elevators in the province. At first the decline was gradual. In 1970, there were 2,750. But toward the end of the century the fall-off had become precipitous. By 2004, there were only 197—and that included new, larger entries in the field. Many of the old elevators have been dismantled or demolished; there was a lot of good lumber in them. Others stand shabbily empty and abandoned.

What had happened? Well, those new, larger

Hero122 / www.en.wikipedia.org

structures—known as inland terminals—had displaced their older brothers. In a sense, you could say that the decline of the traditional elevator began with the internal combustion engine. Towns—and their elevators—had been positioned along the railway at intervals that made sense when grain was hauled in horse-drawn wagons. But trucks could haul longer distances. They made some of the smaller towns—and their elevators—unnecessary.

A more serious blow to the old elevators came when the closure of some branch rail lines and the introduction of large inland terminals situated out in the countryside forced farmers to transport their grain from an even larger radius. From the point of view of the grain companies, one advantage of these new sites was space—more space for railway sidings and bigger trucks. Another was the need for fewer employees who used more efficient technology to operate fewer and larger facilities. Townsfolk might have appreciated the fact that the location of these terminals kept noise and dust well away from their communities. But while larger centres could continue to draw people from the countryside with their businesses and amenities, the loss of a grain elevator was just one more nail in the coffin of a smaller town.

The trend toward inland terminals is part of the story of amalgamations, corporate takeovers and multinationals in the grain business. It is reminiscent of the story the 20th century has to tell about oil companies. In the process the old logos of United Grain Growers and the various wheat pools have faded into history. There are still a few elevators around that are operated by farmer cooperatives, but those of the big players in big business dwarf their operations.

When a branch line closes, so, too, do the adjacent grain elevators.

Obsequies / www.en.wikipedia.org

Both Photos: Clark Saunders

Above: The brand is no more, but cigarette advertising lives on in this Medicine Hat wall mural, uncovered in 2007.

Below: One of two Canadian Pacific locomotives on display at Riverside Veterans' Memorial Park, Medicine Hat

James Marshall. Midcentury visitors arrived a few decades too early to see them.

Nor, for a very different reason, would they have seen the sign on the east wall of the old Pingle's Drug and Book Store, at 627 2nd Street SE. (By the post–Second World War era it was Liggett's Drug Store that was in residence.) Had they seen it, the sign would have instructed them to smoke Sweet Caporal cigarettes. The sign is obviously an old one. The reason it was unseen 60 years ago is that it had long been hidden from view by a building constructed next door. When the next-door building was destroyed by fire in 2007 this "ghost sign" was revealed in nearly pristine condition. Dating from a time when cigarette advertising was both legal and socially acceptable, the sign is bold and uncompromising, covering as it does almost the entire wall of the building—and on the side of a former drug store, no less. Sweet Caps were sold in the Canadian market for 125 years. But you just can't get them any more, so the sign may be doing no harm.

Before the bypass was built, the way out of town for westbound travellers lay across the old, green Finlay Bridge at the foot of 6th Avenue SE. At least, that was the route taken by those who wanted to use the No. 1 Highway. As late as the early 1950s, some chose to travel to Calgary by heading west on the No. 3 as far as Fort McLeod before turning north on the No. 2. The distance was greater, but it included a higher proportion of paved road.

But we are committed to the TCH. Just before it leaves downtown Medicine Hat to cross the South Saskatchewan River on the Finlay Bridge, the old route passes the small Riverside Memorial Park. The two Canadian Pacific diesel locomotives that are a feature of the park were put into service in the 1950s. They stand as a reminder of a time when Canada's highways left something to be desired, and many travellers still chose to take the train.

After crossing the bridge the city route turns west through the old residential area of Riverside on 3rd Street NW. Drivers who want to sample the older highway can avoid finding themselves on the new one by taking Saamis Drive on the right just before the interchange with the current TCH. The drive passes under the new highway before continuing on its way to Redcliff.

Jeffmilner / www.en.wikipedia.org

Peter St. John

Once it has found its way, as it were, the old highway not only parallels the new, it runs along right beside it all the way to the neighbouring town. Redcliff may resent being dismissed as an outlying suburb of Medicine Hat, but its original reasons for existence are similar. Named for the high red shale banks of the nearby South Saskatchewan River, its coal and natural gas drew glass, brick and pottery industries in the early days of its history.

The old highway bends leftward on entering the town centre. After making a right turn at the stop sign at the corner of 3rd Street NE, it continues northward. It bends to the left again as it leaves Redcliff and goes on to parallel the new highway once more.

Pavement continues until the road reaches Range Road 65. At the point where gravel takes over, a blue and white sign—looking like a street sign in deepest suburbia—identifies the route as "Old Trans Canada Hwy". At this point there is little reason to continue on the gravel. The new highway is close at hand. Continuing on it in a northwesterly direction, motorists can rest assured that there is nothing between them and the old highway to their left but the railway embankment. The embankment hides it from view, but should they doubt that the old road is still there, the occasional dust plume sent up by local traffic will assure them that, except for brief intervals during which it wanders a short distance away, the former highway is doing its best to keep in touch.

The present alignment, which wasn't paved until the mid-'50s, crosses some of the most sparsely inhabited terrain of the entire

In Medicine Hat, the TCH passes through an important First Nations archaeological site, miraculously preserved in an urban setting.

The city's name, Medicine Hat, is an English translation of the Siksika word "saamis", which describes the eagle tail feather headdress worn by a medicine man.

The Saamis Teepee, which is adjacent to the highway, is purportedly the world's tallest tipi.

Brian Wolitski / bmwphotos.smugmug.com

As in past decades, coyotes continue to be frequently sighted along southern Alberta's highways.

Coyotes evolved in North America about 1.8 million years ago and have adapted particularly well to living in urban settings.

route across the Prairie Provinces. Between Redcliff and Brooks the only town along the way is Suffield, which has given its name to the Canadian Forces base that covers some of southern Alberta's least promising agricultural territory. The military makes use of a land grant equivalent in size to about two thirds of Prince Edward Island.

Beyond Suffield, as grasshopper-type oil pumps come into view, the old highway diverges somewhat from the new. But as if it could not bear to stay away for long, it comes closer as it approaches Brooks. By turning left from the modern highway onto Provincial Highway 875, motorists arrive in less than a mile at the old highway. Heading southeast from this intersection the old route takes the form of Range Road 134A and is unpaved. But that's okay, because drivers bound for Brooks will want to turn right. In this direction it is Township Road 182A and has a paved surface to offer. Immediately a strange sight greets the traveller: a grove of trees in the midst of bald prairie. This is Tillebrook Provincial Park. It is a pleasant place, but it was not established in time to welcome the weary midcentury motorist; it was not chartered until 1975.

From the park to Brooks, the old road changes name (or rather number) from township to township, but it is well paved the whole way. An irrigation ditch is crossed along the route—an early reminder that Brooks is a place that long ago got into the business of making the desert bloom. The now defunct aqueduct, eight kilometres south of town, is more than a century old. In fact, it was already defunct by the time midcentury visitors had a chance to gaze at it.

Clark Saunders

The old route through town comes in from the southeast. Paralleling the railway line as Township Road 184A, it turns north on 7th Street SE, west on 2nd Avenue E, and finally north again on the main drag, 2nd Street W. North of the town centre it passes a period motel that, like the Satellite in Medicine Hat, derives its name from the space age. Telstar was a communications satellite that in 1962 inspired a British instrumental hit of the same name by a group called The Tornados. The Tel Star (two words) Motor Inn is a two-storey affair that announces its presence with a prominent sign consisting of a spherical object (a satellite, of course) supported in the cleft of three skinny poles surmounted by stars. When this distinctive sign first appeared Neil Armstrong had yet to take one small step for man.

From Brooks to Calgary the Old Highway No. 1 was a longer route in the early 1950s than it is today. That is because the former alignment was a continuation of Brooks' 2nd Street W northward about 17 kilometres to a point beyond the village of Duchess. Today, while the modern route follows the railway, that older north-south stretch is a paved road designated Provincial Highway 873. Irrigation sprinklers along the route provide a less-than-subtle clue as to why this naturally dry area has become so productive.

The old highway passes along the east side of Duchess. No longer PH 873, the pavement continues north as Range Road 144. Where the pavement on the range road ends the route turns west on TR 212 (that's Township 21, Road 2). After it crosses Highway 36 the designation is Provincial Highway 550. It finally reconnects with the new highway just before Bassano. More picturesque than the newer alignment, the old route is beautifully paved today. It would have been just a gravel road when it served as the main east-west route to Calgary.

Crossing the new highway, PH 550 becomes TR 212 again. As it angles north into Bassano this old alignment becomes 11th Street. A block to the west on 5th Avenue near the centre of town, the Midway Motel, in brown and white with a gravel parking lot, is a modest relic of the postwar era. Continuing north on 11th Street will only end in disappointment—and a dead end, as its former roadbed is taken over by the eastbound lanes of the newer four-lane highway. Before travellers have gone that far, it is better to pay attention to the signs directing them back to the modern highway.

Had there been any doubt about it, the

Space Age design is alive and well at the Tel Star Motor Inn in Brooks, Alberta.

Clark Saunders

onward route will provide reminders of the fact that this is cattle country. Breeds like Aberdeen Angus have been found in Canada for as long as 150 years, but the first Charolais did not land in Alberta until 1953 and Simmentals not until more than a decade later. The number of herds of these exotic continental breeds encountered by midcentury motorists would have ranged from few to none.

North of Bassano, the TCH cuts a former right angle and heads west again toward Cluny where another right angle was eliminated as far back as the late 1940s. They may have moved the road, but they haven't moved the mountains. It is just after Cluny and just before descending from a rise that most travellers still get their first glimpse of the Rockies.

South of Cluny near the spot where Provincial Highway 842 crosses the Bow River is a historic site that in the middle years of the last century had not yet received the attention it deserved. Blackfoot Crossing (now a historic park) marks the place where Treaty 7 was signed in 1877. Today, an interpretive centre and other buildings provide displays that shed light on Chief Crowfoot and other 19th-century figures of the Siksika nation (once known as the Blackfoot), as well as the Cree chief Poundmaker. Artifacts relating to earlier peoples who met at this ancient river crossing can also be seen.

Back on the Trans-Canada, another former corner is cut at

If you don't see a coyote near the road, you'll certainly see large domesticated ungulates. Alberta is cattle country!

Canstockphoto / CSP-12846740

Gleichen before the highway turns north again. An old alignment ran straight north from the town on a route that parallels the present one but a short distance east of it. Today, that road begins as PH 547 and becomes Range Road 230. In the days when this was the TCH, it jogged west after a few kilometres to line up with the route of the present highway. All of this was smoothed out in the early '50s.

After it rounds the next bend the TCH turns westward once more before making a very nearly straight run for Calgary. On the way, it passes along the south side of Strathmore. The contrast between what travellers would have seen here in 1965 and what they see today is more than slight. Today the highway is a divided four-lane affair—as it is across the entire province. In 1965, it was two-lane. Today, the highway is flanked by fast-food franchises, motel chains and big box stores; the names of most of these would have been unfamiliar to travellers a half century ago. A population of less than 1,000 in 1965 has grown to more than 13,000. And to a local economy of agriculture, gas and oil, Strathmore has added a second identity as a bedroom suburb of Calgary. The really remarkable thing, though, is that in spite of so much change around it, the highway's route through this area is essentially the same as it was before the Second World War.

Twenty kilometres west at Chestermere the modern highway bends north and west again before entering the city as 16th Avenue NE. This has been the route of the highway since the late 1950s. But before then it simply made a little bend around most of Chestermere Lake before continuing on an alignment that ran into the centre of the city. This road still exists under the title Highway 1A. Those who want to follow it need only watch for the 1A exit at Chestermere, a town that has changed as much as Strathmore has over the years. From a sleepy summer village (the Chestermere Cabin Owners Association was formed in 1959) the place has evolved into a Calgary suburb of oversized, up-market homes and a golf and country club to keep the gentry entertained. Speed boats ply the waters as of yore, but the style of the boats, like that of the community itself, has come a long way since the days when this was a modest country escape for Calgary's middle class.

The approach to Calgary provides travellers with views of its impressive downtown. It may be hard to believe that it was not until

Grapher78 / www.en.wikipedia.org

Above: A plaque in Blackfoot Crossing Historical Park commemorates the 1877 signing of Treaty 7 between the First Nations of what is now southern Alberta and the Canadian government. Crowfoot, chief of the Siksika, is believed to be buried in the park.

Below: The sailboat in Chestermere Lake's logo reflects its early years as a summer retreat

1967 that the Calgary Tower (then the Husky Tower) rose to mark Canada's centennial as the city's tallest structure. Prior to the raising of the tower, Calgary's downtown was not particularly impressive. Today, the tower is dwarfed and hidden by a forest of taller commercial buildings. The growth of downtown Calgary is a reflection of the growth of the city's population: from 180,000 in 1956 to 1.2 million today.

As much as the city has changed, an event that brought summer visitors to Calgary in the 1950s draws them still: the annual Exhibition and Stampede. Now in its second century, the Stampede had already experienced considerable development by the time the Stampede Corral was completed in 1950 and the Stampede Park expanded in 1954. During the same decade the event's profile had reached a point at which it could draw both real royalty (Princess Elizabeth and Prince Philip) and entertainment royalty (Roy Rogers and Walt Disney).

The Exhibition and Stampede had started as separate entities that merged in 1923. By the '50s, Victoria Park had become well established as the venue and pancake breakfasts and the controversial chuck-wagon races had become familiar features of the week each year when the old west came back to Calgary.

In the middle years of the last century, most road traffic coming

Calgary's skyline has mushroomed along with its population. It now has more than six times as many people as it did in 1956.

Canstockphoto/CSP - 6627899

Canstockphoto/CSP - 1470053

from the east to the Stampede—or just passing through town—would have entered the city via what is now Highway 1A. It may be hard to imagine what much of the old route into the city looked like in the early postwar years; urban sprawl has extended far beyond what would have been the city limits in those days. The route becomes 17th Avenue SE and runs through newer suburbs before reaching what was the edge of the city a half century ago. Before the Blackfoot Trail was constructed, 17th Avenue led on to 9th Avenue SE. But today, drivers who want to follow the 1A route will have to stay on 17th Avenue until shortly after it becomes the Blackfoot Trail. The exit to 15th Street SE will get them back to 9th Ave where they can continue their journey westward toward the heart of the city.

Ninth Avenue crosses an older part of town and comes temptingly close to an attraction of bygone days—an attraction that young baby boomers would beg their parents not to miss. Late in the 20th century, the Calgary Zoo became a world-class example of its kind. But in the middle years of that century it was a modest affair confined to St. George's Island in the Bow River. (From 9th Avenue SE it was accessed by a cross street, 12th Street SE. Looking north at the intersection of 9th Avenue and 12th Street today you can see the narrow bridge that leads to the island.) For the average child who visited the zoo 60 years ago, the animals were all well and fine, but what was of real interest were the dinosaurs.

It was in the 1930s that Finnish sculptor John Kanerva designed more than 50 life-size concrete replicas of dinosaurs for the new

The Calgary Stampede takes place every July. At the heart of the 10-day event is the rodeo, one of the world's largest.

Qyd / www.en.wikipedia.org

Natural History Park on the island. (The Alberta badlands were becoming known as a good place to unearth dinosaur fossils, so building models of the creatures just seemed the right thing to do.) For the next few decades, families delighted in the company of the *Stegosaurus*, the *Triceratops*, and their especially scary confrère, *Tyrannosaurus rex*. But eventually they all went the way of the, uh, dinosaur. Not only did later scientific discoveries reveal inaccuracies in some of the models, but in the fullness of time a new and improved Prehistoric Park would open at the zoo on the north side of the river. The old models were rendered obsolete, but one, nicknamed "Dinny", was kept as a memento of the recent past. (In fact, after he became the zoo mascot in 1959, there was really no way to get rid of him.) Boomer kids called him a *Brontosaurus*, but as it turns out, that merely displayed their ignorance. As any six-year-old dinosaur expert today will patiently tell you, he is an *Apatosaurus*. His surroundings have now become the Dorothy Harvie Gardens. If you want to have a look at him without paying the price of admission, cross the 12th Street bridge to St. George's Island and, after leaving your car in the parking lot, walk back a hundred metres or so and peek through the chain link fence. If you're lucky you'll find him browsing among the higher branches of a convenient tree.

Melanie Froese

St. George's Island today. In the 1950s, it was home to dinosaurs—sculptured ones, including a version of *Triceratops*. Today, one remains, an *Apatasaurus*, sequestered in what is now the Dorothy Harvie Gardens on St. George's Island.

Opposite: Bede735 / www.en.wikipedia.org

from CALGARY
– to the BRITISH COLUMBIA
BORDER

Midcentury travellers who had been diverted by the call of the dinosaur could get to the heart of Calgary by re-crossing the 12th Street Bridge and continuing back to 9th Avenue SE. Now part of Highway 1A, until the mid-1950s 9th Avenue was the route of the Trans-Canada Highway. Following it west leads across the Elbow River on an old bridge. Today, as it approaches downtown, 9th Avenue takes on the appearance of a canyon, with the old Palliser Hotel and the Calgary Tower and the train station on the left, all of them backing onto the CPR's mainline. Keep your eyes on the road, though, because this street is no longer friendly to westbound travellers. At 3rd Street SE, 9th Avenue becomes a one-way street coming toward you, and you will be obliged to make a right turn if you want to proceed into the city centre on something approximating the old route.

But for nearly 60 years now, cross-country travellers have been encouraged to follow a route that avoids Calgary's downtown. By staying on the modern TCH at Chestermere, drivers will be guided into the city on an alignment that becomes first 16th Avenue NE and then, after crossing Centre Street, 16th Avenue NW. It is a route that today passes numerous suburbs that were undreamed of in mid-20th century times. But then, as now, traffic would have slowed down after passing the valley through which the Deerfoot Trail now runs.

Since 1964 hot, tired, hungry and thirsty tourists travelling this route have found relief at 219 16th Avenue NE under the sign of Peters' Drive-In. Started by a Dutch immigrant named Gus Pieters, the drive-in has been selling burgers and fries and similar fare on a cash-only basis for a half century. But what the place is really famous for is its milkshakes. There were 30 flavours on offer at last report, and the staff will even mix up to three flavours together for those who just can't make up their minds. Over the years, the parking lot

Calgary Tower

OPPOSITE: Moraine Lake, a glacially-fed lake just west of Old No. 1 (and the TCH) between Banff and Lake Louise.

www.en.wikipedia.org

Canstockphoto/CSP - 0124225

The Bow River at Bowness Park in northwest Calgary.

has expanded to include shaded picnic tables, and a double line of vehicles can be accommodated at the drive-through, one on each side of the building.

Farther west on 16th Avenue NW (Highway 1) between Banff Trail and the Crowchild Trail (Highway 1A) motorists arrive at Motel Village. Set in a triangle bordered by these three streets, and with McMahon Stadium on the University of Calgary campus as a close neighbour, the village owes its origins to the construction of a new highway to the mountains. The new TCH was built in the late '50s, the stadium opened in 1960, and a collection of motels sprang up at about the same time. In those days they were "independents". Today they all belong to one chain or another.

Our exploration of the old highway will take us out of town on No. 1A, but vehicles following the newer route will soon find themselves in the hollow that is Bowness. Until 1963, when it was absorbed by the city, Bowness was a separate town. It retains its distinctive character today. As the new highway route wended its way through the place, motels were built as well. Some have disappeared, but a few remain.

But to return to the old highway: from Motel Village, the old route out of town is by way of Highway No. 1A. It is a road that has been known by a variety of names. Part of it originated as the old Banff Coach Road, otherwise known as the Banff Trail. (In fact, before it merges with the freeway, the short street along the east side of Motel Village still goes by the latter name.) When it was first paved in the 1930s, it became "the highway to Banff." In 1971, the section

western alberta

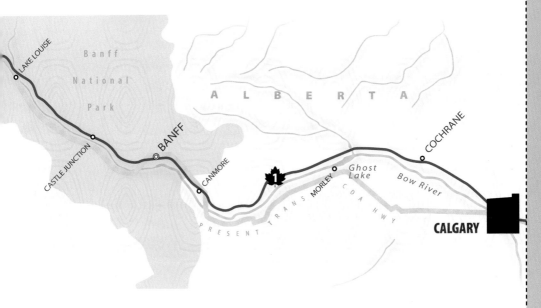

Map: Dawn Huck

DRIVING THE OLD ROUTE FROM CALGARY TO CANMORE—NOW DESIGNATED AS HIGHWAY 1A—CONVEYS AN IMPRESSION OF ROAD TRAVEL IN CANADA OVER HALF A CENTURY AGO. THE SECTION OF OLD HIGHWAY IN BANFF NATIONAL PARK NOW GOES BY THE NAME "BOW VALLEY PARKWAY".

Growing tall and straight, *Pinus contorta,* the lodgepole pine, was used for millennia by First Nations for tipi structures and travois that were pulled by dogs and later horses. In recent years, in both Alberta and B.C., vast swaths of mature trees have been destroyed by pine beetle infestations. Though the pine beetle (and the blue fungus it creates, which is what actually kills the trees) are endemic in pine forests, biologists believe that climate change has greatly exacerbated the spread of the beetle. At right, a young lodgepole pine.

ALBERTA PROVINCIAL TREE

LODGEPOLE PINE

Canstockphoto/CSP - 10104799

Ryan Sardachuk / Fastlane Illustration

A rendering of Eamon's Bungalow Camp in Calgary as it looked in midcentury, complete with a 1956 Chevrolet Bel Air. A new LRT station is scheduled for the site.

of highway within the city became part of one of Calgary's early attempts to create a freeway: the Crowchild Trail. Call it what you will, a six-lane thoroughfare now leads traffic out of town (a longer process every year) past the University of Calgary. It was not until 1966 that the campus declared its independence from the University of Alberta in Edmonton. Since then, it has grown prodigiously, and the surrounding suburbs with it. A line of the city's light rapid transit (LRT) running down the middle of the freeway is just one more feature that would mystify a time-traveller returning from the 1950s to this part of the country. It would indeed have been "country" then; it is "country" no longer.

As Calgary's LRT expands northwestward with the city, a new station is in the works at a location just past 1A's interchange with another freeway, Stoney Trail. The station's setting has a history. On this spot, beginning in 1949, the late Roy Eamon built first a drive-in restaurant, then a Texaco gas station, and finally a 12-unit motel called Eamon's Bungalow Camp. Offering what he called "one-stop tourist service", Roy had created a landmark on the old highway. Unfortunately, by the mid-1960s, the new highway had killed it.

But the vertical tower sign and the Art Moderne–style garage with its curved stucco walls somehow survived. When civic leaders came to plan the Tuscany LRT station on the site in 2012, citizens with an appreciation of midcentury architecture and a sentimental attachment to the place organized a campaign to have the sign and building stored for future use in the hope that the new station could incorporate these precious relics from a fast-fading period of history. As of this writing, the building is scheduled for demolition, but the sign is to be incorporated into the neighbouring Rocky Ridge Park and Ride lot. There are also plans to add an interpretive panel outlining the history of the tourist stop.

As Highway 1A extends beyond the city limits and is reduced first to four lanes and then at Cochrane, to two, it takes on more and more the look and feel of the meandering transcontinental highway it once was. Mind you, Cochrane itself has expanded beyond all recognition. The population statistics themselves tell the story: from 707 in 1956 to 17,580 in 2011. This is an even greater population explosion than Strathmore, on the other side of Calgary, has experienced. It suggests that people looking for a place to live within commuting distance of the city figure they may as well find something with a mountain view.

In 1963, long before the suburbs of Cochrane had wrapped themselves around the southern slopes of the big hill that marks the approach to the town from the east, Edward McCourt had enjoyed that view. Adding yet another name for the old route—the Bow Valley Trail—he allowed that it was "familiarly called the Banff Trail". Writing in *The Road Across Canada* just a few years after the new highway had bypassed Cochrane 15 kilometres to the south of the town, he went on:

> *In some respects the old highway is even more scenic than the new—at certain points it affords a broader panorama embracing the entire sweep of the Bow Valley and the mountains beyond. One of the finest views in all Canada is that from the turn-out at the top of the great hill above the village of Cochrane twenty miles west of Calgary—a magnificent expanse of river, valley, foothills, mountains, and overarching sky juxtaposed in a flawlessly balanced harmony, so flawless as to suggest a deliberately contrived artistic improvement on nature.*

MacKay's Ice Cream Parlour in Cochrane has been serving homemade ice cream since 1948.

McCourt's rhapsody continues, but that is perhaps enough to give the flavour of it. And speaking of flavour, down in the valley where Cochrane began, MacKay's Ice

Courtesy of www.mackaysicecream

Cream Parlour is ready to refresh the long-distance traveller and the day tripper from Calgary just as it has been since opening in 1948. That was the year James and Christina Mackay (even the website can't decide whether it's MacKay or Mackay) introduced homemade ice cream into their general store at 220 1st Street West. Soon everything general had gone and only the ice cream remained. Over the years, new flavours have been introduced. Dill pickle was one that (surprisingly) came and (less surprisingly) went. But business continues to be brisk. The "J. A. MacKay General Merchant" sign inside is a link with the past. But under the guidance of a third generation of MacKay descendants, the parlour is also very much a thing of the present.

West of Cochrane the old highway passes the Ghost Lake reservoir. Part of the Bow River system, the lake was formed in 1929. Though the dam that created it was built with power generation in mind, the lake has always attracted people who enjoy fishing for varieties of trout and whitefish.

As it runs through the lands of the Stoney First Nation, the highway's lack of shoulders has prompted the placing of signs that read, "Watch for Pedestrians on Highway." Good advice. Pedestrian sightings are not infrequent.

In the heart of Stoney country stands the church of the Morley-

The McDougall Stoney Mission Church built in 1875 is southern Alberta's oldest surviving Protestant church and the oldest remaining structure in the Bow Valley.

Clark Saunders

Alexis Harrison / www.en.wikipedia.org

ville Historic Mission. Built in the 1870s by the father-and-son Methodist missionary team of George and John McDougall, the mission had a wide influence until the church closed for regular worship in 1921. Aside from the addition of a cairn that was erected six years later, the site received little attention until a restoration was undertaken in 1950. Since then, visitors have rightly appreciated the work of the McDougall Stoney Mission Society, which has done much to spruce the place up. For many years now, a fenced path has led across a meadow strewn with wildflowers to the white-and-green painted church and its little graveyard. A small lake to the south and the mountains to the west complete an idyllic scene.

West of Morley the speed limit drops to 80 km/h and just 65 on the curves. Since the midcentury motorist drove through these parts, the Kananaskis country to the south has seen considerable development. In 1963, Edward McCourt and his wife (the nameless Mrs. McCourt) took a side trip into what was then the Kananaskis Forest Reserve. The forestry road was rough in spots, but the scenery, so far undiscovered by most, inspired another of McCourt's superlatives. The area was in his view "one of the most magnificent and least cluttered mountain and lake regions in all Canada." The clutter would come later.

Motorists heading west on either Highway 1 or Highway 1A find that the foothills give way to mountains with an impressive suddenness. On the old highway progress is slower, and around Exshaw the road runs right past a number of industrial plants that the new

West of Calgary, the TCH takes travellers near Kananaskis country, including what was in midcentury called the Kananaskis Forest Reserve. In later years, it became Kananaskis Provincial Park and then was renamed Lougheed Provincial Park, for the premier of Alberta from 1971 to 1985.

Jerry Kautz

Above: The Rocky Mountain bighorn sheep is the provincial mammal of Alberta.

Below: The view outside Canmore

highway views only distantly from the other side of the Bow Valley. Graymont's lime and limestone, Lafarge's cement plant, and the sand and gravel of Burnco Rock Products are set amid the mountain majesty. Unfortunately some of their work involves sending smoke into the pristine mountain air. Around Exshaw a motorist is as likely to encounter a sign that warns, "Blasting No Stopping" as one that urges caution because of the proximity of mountain sheep.

As it approaches Canmore, Highway 1A passes under the present TCH and, still with the moniker "Bow Valley Trail", becomes Canmore's older bypass. This is a route that has had modern hotels built along it and feels like part of the town. But there is a still older route that passes through the town centre on the opposite side of the CPR line to the left. On the way westward out of town, Highway 1A joins the new highway at an interchange and effectively disappears as a distinct entity for a while.

Canmore has gone up-market since its early days as a mining town and its later period as Banff's poor sister, just outside the park. Its growth has been only slightly less dramatic than Cochrane's—from 1,379 in 1956 to 12,317 in 2013. Its expansion has been accompanied by a boom in real estate prices, which has put most properties out of reach for the average income earner. Sixty years ago people generally did not come to Canmore to ski or to get married. Today, they do.

Peter St. John

Peter St. John

Travellers are truly in the mountains by this point. If our old friend Edward McCourt was bored by eastern Saskatchewan, he felt oppressed by the mountains. They seemed to have slipped in behind him and cut off his retreat. The Three Sisters, the mountain that dominates Canmore, he described as "beautiful but sinister". And what would he have made of Ha Ling Peak if he had heard of it?

When McCourt was passing through in 1963 people were calling it "Chinaman's Peak". In fact, that is what they would call it for another 34 years. Situated at the northwest end of Mount Lawrence Grassi (which in turn rises northwest of the Three Sisters), the origin of the name of this peak is a story with variations. The gist of it is that near the end of the 19th century a Chinese cook in Canmore climbed the peak in record time on a bet and planted a flag at the summit. When people doubted his story, he did it again—but with a bigger flag. A century later, the "Chinaman" title had become offensive. As well, it was noted that when a mountain was named after someone with European origins it seemed customary to give it the individual's name. It was high time this double standard was abolished. The cook-mountain-climber appears to have been named Ha Ling, and since 1997 the peak has carried his name. We can hope that that will end the matter, but be advised that the supporters of another cook named Lee Poon have come in with a dissenting opinion. So stay tuned.

Above: Tunnel Mountain Road loops from Banff Avenue around the mountain. The CPR initially planned a tunnel here, but found it cheaper to go around. The road allows a grand view of the Bow River and the hoodoos on the mountain slope.

Below: Banff Park Museum National Historic Site. The 1903 log structure is characteristic of early park buildings.

Clark Saunders

After Highway 1 gives up its separate identity just beyond Canmore, it is a matter of only a minute or two before the quaint stone and half-timbered gates of Banff National Park come into view. When Canada's first national park was created, it was really the railway that gave it birth and the railway that got people there. But as highways improved after the Second World War, more and more people arrived by car. Banff Avenue, reached today by an exit from the TCH, approximates the traditional route into the town of Banff.

When it arrives at the heart of the town site it bends to the left and becomes Banff's main drag. Midsummer traffic was heavy and slow here in the 1950s. It still is.

It is unusual on this side of the Atlantic to find a museum that is itself a building of historical interest. But at the foot of Banff Avenue on the near side of the old stone bridge that carries traffic across the Bow River stands what is now designated as the Banff Park Museum National Historic Site. Built in 1903, it is the oldest federal building in a national park. It is an eye-catching structure distinguished by the use of Douglas fir in its cross-log construction, by the way natural light streams through its large windows and the clerestory lantern at its peak, and by its bracketed veranda and the cantilevered truss system that supports the second storey. Its style has been said to reflect the design of smaller railway stations across the country.

Canada's national parks system began in 1885 when Banff National Park was established around the Cave and Basin Hot Springs. Legend says that a bear seeking its healing waters alerted early travellers to its existence.

Barbara Endres

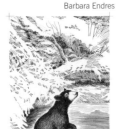

Peter St. John

Both inside and out the museum appears much as it would have done to visitors in 1920 or 1960. The interior features examples of the taxidermist's art displayed in cases that reflect the style of museums a hundred years ago. And as for the exterior, the dark brown paint that was applied in the 1970s has been removed so that the building looks as it would have looked to both midcentury travellers and the first visitors who walked through its doors.

Of course, another thing that has not changed around Banff is the mountain backdrop. But easy means of getting to the tops of some of these peaks have been added. Mount Norquay's chair lift, which claims to be the second oldest in North America, dates from 1948, while the gondola lift on Sulphur Mountain (one of the first in Canada) began hauling groups of tourists up to the summit ridge in 1959.

Motorists in search of the next leg of old highway will have little choice but to follow the four-lane TCH for about seven kilometres after leaving Banff. (The Vermilion Lakes Drive running along the south side of the highway is a vestige of the old road, but it comes to a dead end.) A long section of IA then shows up on the right as the Bow Valley Parkway.

A vestige of Old No. 1 West forms today's Vermilion Lakes Drive, affording magnificent views of the wetlands with Mount Rundle in the distance.

Peter St. John

gonna name a mountain

Brian Wolitski

ONE OF THE HAND-SOMEST, MOST DISTINCTIVE AND MOST EASILY RECOGNIZABLE MOUNTAINS in Banff National Park is located about halfway between Banff and Lake Louise. In the postwar years, baby boomers and their parents learned to call it Mount Eisenhower.

But as a boy I remember thinking it looked an awful lot like a castle.

I was not alone in thinking so. Others had had this great thought before me.

James Hector for one. The explorer, impressed with the fortress-like appearance of the mountain's east end and southern flank, had named it Castle Mountain in 1858. And so it was known for the better part of a century.

But then in 1946, General Dwight D. Eisenhower visited Ottawa. (He would not become president until 1953.) The government of W. L. McKenzie King thought it right and fitting to honour the former Supreme Allied Commander who had recently overseen the liberation of Western Europe. Scotland had given him the use of an apartment in a castle. Surely Canada could do better than that. How about naming a mountain after him? Well, it seemed like a good idea at the time.

At least the federal government thought so. The government of Alberta begged to differ. The Albertans were incensed that Ottawa would presume not only to name but to *re*-name one of their mountains without even a pretense of consultation. Efforts to have the federal action reversed began almost immediately.

It was not until 1979 that a compromise was reached. The mountain reverted to its original name, but the title Eisenhower Peak was assigned to the semi-detached promontory that faces eastward—the first part of the mountain that a traveller sees when driving toward British Columbia.

The name may have gone though a couple of changes, but the motorist's experience in driving past the mountain is as it was. As you approach from the east it appears to stand in splendid isolation. Then, as you drive along its southern flank, especially on the TCH, changing perspectives make the mountain appear to stretch out like an expanding accordion. The play of light on rock has a way of changing colour after the first pinkish impression. Whatever name the mountain goes by (and perhaps, like T.S. Eliot's cats, the mountain itself knows its real name), it is a geographical feature that leaves a lasting image on the inward eye.

Before leaving the new road, though, there are opportunities to see some of the signs that point like wooden fingers to some of the taller mountains. The signs are inscribed with the mountains' names and elevations. In the 1960s, their heights were indicated in feet; since the '70s, the unit of measurement has been metres.

Immediately after leaving the new highway, travellers become aware of the things that make the parkway different: cattle grids, the lack of shoulders, trees crowding the edge of the road rather than keeping a respectful distance as they do on the main route. At times the east- and west-bound lanes diverge from one another. A long and winding road, the park-way offers occasional views of the blue-green Bow River on the left. Cyclists are a common sight on this route today, but they would have been a rarity in the middle of the 20th century. In fact, back then the appearance of cyclists might have prompted a motorist to wonder what had possessed them.

The occasional hostelry of one sort or another can be found along the way. The oldest of them is located at the trailhead to Johnston Canyon. It occupies a site that during the First World War served as a camp for "enemy aliens", Canadian residents whose home countries were now at war with His Majesty's dominions. These men were put to work building the highway from Banff to Lake Louise. After two summers, they had only 12 kilometres of road to show for their efforts.

In the late 1920s, Walter and Marguerite Camp began a business on this spot. Their family continues to run it today. Taking over an existing teahouse, they added an Esso gas station and, in the 1930s, eight cabins. The Esso station was the first in the park, and the cabins were the park's first accommodations that were not owned by the CPR. Walter shared his love of the area by giving lectures to the guests from 1932 until the year before his death in 1979. Known in its earlier days as the Johnston Canyon Bungalow Camp, the accom-

Courtesy Pauline Kaill

Midcentury visitors to national parks were more likely to see bears and less likely to heed warnings not to feed them.

Clark Saunders

Above: The old office building at Johnston Canyon Resort, which has been going strong since the early 1930s.

Opposite: Lake Louise, photographed in 1965. Today, with climate change, the Victoria Glacier is much diminished.

modations trade today under the name of the Johnston Canyon Resort. The old office building, cabins and even an Esso gas pump can still be seen among more recent additions to the operation.

The parkway affords a very different view of Castle Mountain from what is seen from the TCH. From the new highway the mountain appears surrounded by space. From the Parkway it rises up ahead of you, framed by the trees that line the sides of the road.

As the parkway and the modern highway approach the mountain with barely a kilometre between them, each comes to its own intersection with Highway 93. The point of connection with the Number 93 has gone by a number of names over the years: Eisenhower Forks, Eisenhower Junction, Castle Mountain, Castle Junction. And Highway 93, which leads south via Radium Hot Springs to the Number 3, was numbered "1B" in the 1950s. Presumably that was because it was the route that transcontinental motor traffic chose if it wanted to avoid as much as possible the long gravel roads that lay in wait along the No. 1 route in British Columbia.

Today those who travel the parkway will find themselves delivered back to the TCH at the commercial centre of Lake Louise Village. But who would come so close to one of Canada's most famous beauty spots and not stay on the parkway as it crosses the highway and magically turns into Lake Louise Drive? A climb of 10 minutes or so should be enough to get a car up to the lake itself.

The CPR and the TCH have never made it to Lake Louise. The gradient is far too steep for a regular rail line to consider, although a narrow-gauge tramway carried tourists up from Lake Louise Station until it was abandoned in 1930. As for the road, it does little to advance the cause of motorists whose aim is to travel east or west. After doing what they came to do at Lake Louise, tourists just turn around and go back down to the highway again.

There was a time, though, when after passing the road to Moraine Lake and shortly before reaching the Lake Louise Parking lot, motorists would watch for a road, sometimes designated as more "1A," leading to a cairn and interpretive sign. These indicated the

Peter St. John

Gorgo / www.en.wikipedia.org

Chateau Lake Louise, shown here reflected in the water of the lake, was built at the turn of the last century by the Canadian Pacific Railway to entice moneyed travellers to take the train. Midcentury travellers arriving by car would have found it strictly a summer place. It wasn't until 1982 that the hotel became a year-round resort.

continental divide and the boundary between Alberta and British Columbia. At one time the spot was marked as well by a wooden arch spanning the road. What makes the place of particular interest is that a stream actually divides at this spot, with some of its droplets heading toward the Pacific while others are bound for Hudson Bay. Alas (from the point of view of the motoring public), the road has been closed to vehicles since the 1990s. Today only pedestrians with the time and energy to do it can make their way to this significant spot.

Some things about Lake Louise have changed over the years. Parking lots have proliferated. Chateau Lake Louise, the park's iconic hotel, has spawned arcades with more shops and services. But the walk from the original parking lot still takes visitors along the familiar Louise Creek that carries the lake's overflow down to the Bow River. And the view at the top of the short path still takes people's breath away.

After tearing themselves away (as eventually they must do), travellers will find themselves back down the hill and heading west on the Trans-Canada Highway. Those bound for the Columbia Icefields, Jasper and other points north will shortly say good-bye as they veer off onto Highway 93, while those destined for British Columbia stay on the No. 1. Until the late '50s, the pavement ended at this divide; both highways were gravel-surfaced from this point. Today, not only are they both paved, but also significant improvements, including a new bridge, are being made on the TCH as it approaches the BC boundary.

Opposite: Courtesy Of Three Valley Lake Chateau

from the

BRITISH COLUMBIA
BORDER *- to*
KAMLOOPS

A single imaginary line across Kicking Horse Pass signifies a number of things. Running north and south, it marks the continental divide, indicates the boundary between Alberta and British Columbia, and divides Banff National Park from Yoho National Park.

When the CPR chose Kicking Horse Pass as its route through the Rockies, the decision was made despite the fact that the grade required on the slope leading down toward Field, British Columbia, was double the normal limit. In fact, at 4.5 per cent, it was said to be the steepest stretch of rail on a regular rail line in North America. Extra locomotives were needed to push trains up what is still called the Big Hill. Going downhill, the hope was that specially installed spur lines would divert runaway trains before they crashed into something. The completion of spiral tunnels in 1909 enabled trains to negotiate a much safer grade by travelling through two mountains.

Today, the entrances to the tunnels can be seen from a viewpoint on the Trans-Canada Highway. What travellers do not always realize is that when the railway abandoned the old line, the former rail bed was available for road construction. The Big Hill became, and has remained, the route not of train but of motor vehicle traffic. The exact roadway may have moved slightly—westbound travellers can see signs of a disused bridge on the left near the summit—but its basic path is as it has been for decades.

After its long descent, the highway leads to Field across a surprisingly flat stretch of terrain. Not far to the north are such tourist draws as the world-renowned Burgess Shale, Emerald Lake and Takakkaw Falls. Field itself, however, is a small village. No longer in serious business as a railway town, it caters to the tourist trade. Although it is in British Columbia, it is a roadside Travel Alberta Visitor Information Centre that prompts traffic to stop here.

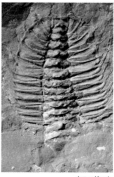

Jerry Kautz

Above: The fossil of a trilobite, an extinct marine creature found in abundance in the Mount Stephen's Burgess Shale formation near Field.

Opposite: Three Valley Gap west of Revelstoke was a modest tourist stop in the 1950s. Today, greatly expanded, it boasts up-to-the-minute resort facilities as well as a heritage ghost town, where visitors can view restored buildings, vintage automobiles and period railway cars.

Courtesy of Three Valley Lake Chateau & Heritage Ghost Town

Peter St. John

The gatehouse at Emerald Lake Lodge. The largest of Yoho National Park's many lakes, Emerald Lake, located just off the TCH, is one of the park's jewels.

Today's Park Bridge, completed in 2007, helped replace a dangerous stretch of highway.

According to a roadmap of the time, in 1950, motorists would not encounter a foot of pavement between the B.C.–Alberta boundary and Revelstoke. Five years later, of that entire route, only a few kilometres of highway west of Yoho Park's west gate were paved. By 1960, pavement extended from the provincial boundary to Golden and beyond, but for decades after that little was done to improve the winding mountain road from Field to Golden. In fact, it became known as one of the most dangerous sections of the TCH in the country. By the turn of the 21st century, it was averaging 140 accidents a year. Finally the provincial and federal governments agreed to spend nearly a billion dollars on the 26 kilometres that run from the park gate to Golden. The result is a beautiful four-lane stretch of highway threading its way through the canyon of the Kicking Horse River. The centrepiece of this project is the 90-metre-high Park Bridge. When B.C. Premier Gordon Campbell attended the ribbon cutting in 2007, he drove across the structure in a '57 Chevy. Finally, 50 years after that car was new, the highway was one the province and country could be proud of.

The road may be vastly improved, but the way into Golden is still down the so-called Ten Mile Hill. At the top of this six per cent grade, trucks are still required to check their brakes. As an added precaution, a runaway lane partway down is provided in case the brakes should fail. Closer to Golden, drivers still encounter some sharp turns and bits of two-lane highway with chain-mail curtains hanging from the roadside cliffs to mitigate the effects of falling rock.

www.th.gov.bc.ca

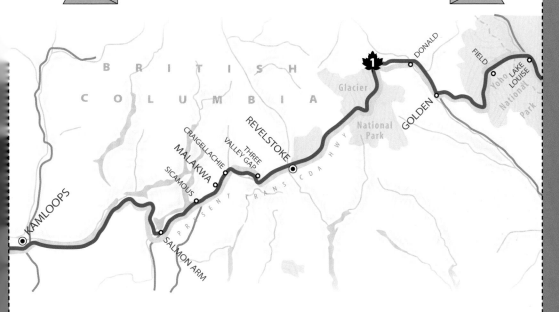

Map: Dawn Huck

VERY LITTLE OF THE HIGHWAY IN THIS PART OF B.C. WAS PAVED UNTIL THE LATE 1950S. THE LONG LOOP OF THE BIG BEND (SEE MAP, PAGE 130) WAS PARTICULARLY DAUNTING AND DISCOURAGED ALL BUT THE MOST INTREPID OF TRAVELLERS. ALL THAT WOULD CHANGE WITH THE COMPLETION OF THE ROGERS PASS SECTION OF THE TCH.

BRITISH COLUMBIA PROVINCIAL FLOWER

PACIFIC FLOWER

Canstockphoto/CSP - 201810

The Pacific dogwood, *Cornus nuttallii,* was adopted as British Columbia's floral emblem in 1956. A tree that grows six to eight meters in height, it flowers in April and May and attracts attention in the fall with its bright red berries and brilliant foliage.

At the spot where the Kicking Horse River flows into the Columbia in the Rocky Mountain Trench, the town of Golden came to life late in the 19th century. Originally, the lumber industry and the CPR drove its economy. Later, its position at the junction of the TCH and Highway 95 added another reason for its existence, namely the feeding, watering and gassing-up of highway travellers. The Trans-Canada runs along a well-established route here, but it was not until after the completion of the Rogers Pass section of the Number 1 Highway that services began to multiply on the strip that skirts the northeast edge of town. Of the restaurants along the service road, it is probably the A&W that has the longest history, one that stretches back to the '60s. With the next filling stations 150 kilometres away in Revelstoke, gas has always been a top-selling commodity in Golden, and never at bargain basement prices.

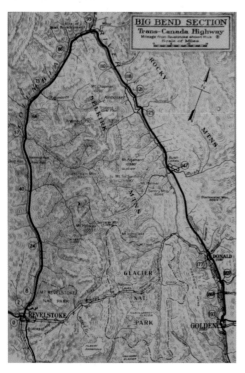

In the 1940s and '50s, driving west of Golden, B.C. meant taking a very long and sometimes arduous detour, the Big Bend Highway, north along the Columbia River and around the Selkirk Mountains.

Until 1962, Golden marked the beginning of what some called the longest detour in the world, the Big Bend Highway. Built as a Depression-era make-work project and opened in 1940, the Big Bend was named for a long loop of the Columbia River. The road followed the river as it flowed away to the north before bending south again and passing through Revelstoke.

In 1941, the new road was designated Highway 1 in recognition of its role as a link in a transnational route. But the Big Bend hardly lived up to the numerical distinction. It was a narrow road with an oil-on-sand surface that deteriorated quickly and required frequent attention. In winter it was closed. In summer, its 305 kilometres took seven hours to drive. The route took motorists up steep grades, over runoffs from melting snow, and past the ominous sight of the rusting wrecks of abandoned vehicles. Not surprisingly it attracted little tourist traffic.

As the Big Bend Highway, the route was never paved, but the modern paved TCH follows the path of the old road as far as the little sawmilling community of Donald. A former divisional point on the CPR, Donald was the spot where the railway (and later the TCH) made its first crossing of the Columbia River. In its early days the village was the site of the rustic St. Stephen's Church. Midcentury travellers would have passed it—but not at Donald. In 1902 it had been moved to Field where it remained until 1965.

At Donald, the railway turned westward to begin its climb up to Rogers Pass, while the old

Brian Wolitski / bmwphotos.smugmug.com

highway continued its northbound route. Today, explorers who want a taste of the old Big Bend will see signs of it on the east (right) side of the TCH as they pass the weigh station just before Donald, but there is no access to it at this point. It is Donald Road—on the right, a few hundred metres farther on—that leads into the village and to the old gravel road. Mounted on top of a stop sign a conventional white-on-green street sign marks the intersection of "Donald Rd" with "Big Bend Hwy". Those who make a left turn here will be led to Donald's northern extremity and then across a narrow bridge over a tributary of the Columbia. At this point, the old highway's modern designation becomes the Bush Forest Service Road. Drivers may want to go a little farther—far enough to enjoy the remote Marl Creek Provincial Park. But be advised: the chances of a logging truck coming barreling down the road toward you are significant. In any case, driving the entire Big Bend is no longer possible. Its northern reaches lie under Kinbasket Lake, a body of water that was vastly expanded by the construction of the Mica Dam in 1973. But another opportunity to travel a bit of the old Big Bend Highway awaits you on the other side of the Selkirk Mountains.

By the early 1950s, thought was being given to an all-season route that would run, not around the Selkirks, but through them. In 1956, it was decided to follow the railway's lead of 70 years earlier and build a new highway over Rogers Pass. When this stretch of road was completed six years later, it reduced the driving distance between Golden and Revelstoke to less than

Above: Mountain fauna: a cow moose and her and calf.

Below: Decision time in Donald, B.C. Turn left and you'll get a taste of the old Big Bend Highway.

Clark Saunders

half of the length of the Big Bend—from more than 300 kilometres to fewer than 150. Although the new route did not go nearly as far north as the old one, it still includes the most northerly point on the entire TCH.

The Selkirks had presented the CPR with an almost insuperable obstacle in the 1880s. But the daunting challenge of laying rail across this avalanche-prone range with its seemingly bottomless ravines was met in amazingly short order. The rail line was completed in an astonishing four years after Major Albert Bowman Rogers immortalized himself by blazing the trail. The rate of loss of life from avalanches during the early years of rail travel was reduced with the completion of the Connaught Tunnel in 1916. The revision of the CPR route that came with the building of the tunnel freed up some old rail right-of-way. Surveyors took advantage of this when the highway was seeking a path over Rogers Pass more than 40 years later.

Created in 1886, Glacier National Park had been accessible only by rail until 1962 when the highway was completed. Today most of the few buildings in the park are clustered around the park

The Rogers Pass. The "shed" structure protects the Discovery Centre from more than two metres of snow that fall annually in the pass.

Peter St. John

headquarters near the summit of the pass. Among them, both with steeply sloped green roofs, are the boarded-up Glacier Park Lodge and a disused gas station. Between these two semi-derelicts, in front of the Discovery Centre and gift shop, stand two of the howitzers that the Royal Canadian Horse Artillery fires to trigger controlled avalanches. These are among the third generation of such weapons to be used for this peaceful purpose. The big guns, together with a series of snow sheds along the route as it follows the Illecillewaet River toward Revelstoke, are the motorist's best defence against snow slides.

The summit of the pass, about a kilometre west of the park headquarters, can be reached by highway or by the Abandoned Rails Trail, an easy hike that is even accessible to wheelchairs. There, beside a picnic area, stands a memorial to those who were killed by an avalanche in 1910—the disaster that galvanized authorities into the action that led to the building of the Connaught Tunnel. Near the memorial stands a monument consisting of two simple arches that interlock at right angles to each other. This is the structure that commemorates the opening of the Rogers Pass section of the Trans-Canada Highway and the virtual completion of the highway as a whole on September 3, 1962.

The Rogers Pass section of the highway has turned out to be a boon to many, but the ceremony that day was so dogged by problems that the more than usually superstitious among those present might have seen them as bad omens. Prime Minister John Diefenbaker and the other speakers were rendered at times inaudible by a defective sound system. The remarks by an official from Saskatchewan left the impression that he thought he was in Quebec. "O Canada" had to be dispensed with because the bus bringing the band instruments got lost; it managed to arrive in time for the playing of "God Save the Queen" at the conclusion of the program. Conspicuous by his absence was B.C. premier W.A.C. Bennett, who had pre-empted the event by staging his own ribbon cutting at a spot about 13 kilometres east of Revelstoke a month earlier. On that occasion he referred to the road as "B.C. Highway No. 1." Today a roadside cairn marks the spot.

Both images: Clark Saunders

Above: An avalanche cannon in Rogers Pass, used to break up the snow in winter before it can thunder down and cover the road.

Below: The monument marking the completion of the TCH in 1962.

Peter St. John

Revelstoke from above. The completion of the TCH in 1962 eased access to the region, bringing in more tourists. Today, skiing is an important boon to the local economy.

But an all-weather road across Canada—at least all of Western Canada—had been completed. What westbound motorists encountered that September is essentially what they find today, more than a half century later. They would have approached Revelstoke, as drivers still do, by means of a long descent reminiscent of the eastern approach to Golden.

Before the new highway opened in 1962, Revelstoke marked the western terminus of the Big Bend Highway. Today this end of that old road features intermittent paving. As Highway 23, it runs all the way north to Mica Dam. Those who have no wish to drive 135 kilometres in order to see it, but who would enjoy being impressed by a mighty rush of water, can drive just three kilometres up Highway 23 to the Revelstoke Dam. Shortly before reaching it, motorists will pass a gate that can be closed when further travel up this road is not advised. Nature still likes to throw her weight around in these parts.

The route of the TCH through Revelstoke has changed little since Rogers Pass was opened to traffic; vehicles still cross the Columbia on the bridge that was part of that highway project. The inauguration of the new highway vastly increased the number of cross-country travellers who came through town and the number of businesses catering to tourists increased accordingly. In the town centre, two motels that opened the same year as the new highway are still in business. Needless to say, both the Alpine Motel and the Powder Springs Inn (which started life as McGregor's Motel) have undergone significant upgrades in the last half century.

Having crossed the Columbia twice and traversed the mighty Selkirks between the crossings, the CPR and TCH continue westward through the Monashee Mountains by way of Eagle Pass. Driving in that direction today, motorists will find that twinning of the highway is being undertaken. They may also notice that this stretch passes a relic of a previous alignment in the form of an old orange rainbow-shaped bridge.

Just as the new highway benefitted businesses in Revelstoke, it had an impact on a modest tourist stop at Three Valley Gap, 19 kilometres west of town. It was in 1956 that a young couple named

Courtesy Of Three Valley Gap

Gordon and Ethel Bell bought some lakeshore property at the east end of Three Valley Lake. Before long they had opened a small motel, restaurant and gift shop. But soon their other interests took over. They took on the task of rescuing derelict buildings that were slated for demolition and transporting them to their property where they gradually took on the look of a historic town. One of their salvage operations involved St. Stephen's Church—the same church that started out in Donald and was moved to Field. The Bells showed up in 1965 just when it was due to be demolished. Another building they saved was the old Craigellachie schoolhouse. An interest in trains added rolling stock to their site. Over the years, tourist accommodations and facilities were expanded, with the addition of live entertainment, an antique car museum and a railway roundhouse. The place bears little resemblance to the tourist stop by the side of the road that some recall from more than 50 years ago. But Gordon and Ethel's descendants just keep expanding on their dream.

Today, the stretch of highway between here and Sicamous has become a kind of family tourist destination, with one roadside attraction following another. But in the early '60s, there was one stop by the road waiting for Trans-Canada travellers to start pouring in—The Enchanted Forest. Overnight it became one of those places that had children begging their parents to stop. *(Please, Dad, can we? Pleeeeze!)* Officially opened to the public on July 1, 1960, The Enchanted Forest consisted of one building and a giant walk-in mushroom. By 1962, when Rogers Pass was opened and the castle and candy-cane house had been added to the Forest's enticements, all those nagging kids were beginning to have an impact. That year, an estimated 10 per cent of passing vehicles stopped there.

Above: The Three Valley Gap resort today. Midcentury visitors would have found a small motel.

Below: Attractions along the TCH in eastern B.C. include the giant mushroom at The Enchanted Forest.

Clark Saunders

Like Three Valley Gap, The Enchanted Forest was a family business, although in this case two families have been involved. Doris and Ernest Needham from Revelstoke were looking for a place where Doris could indulge her hobby of making handcrafted fairy-tale figurines of cement. The locale was very isolated when they found the spot they were looking for. But that changed with coming of the new highway. As the number of visitors grew, so did what had started as a retirement project for the Needhams. Eventually, feeling that the place had outgrown their energy, Ernest and Doris sold it. Since 1970, it has been in the hands of Rocky and Juliet Ehlers and their family.

If the completion of the highway through Rogers Pass made The Enchanted Forest not merely a viable enterprise but a going concern, it also brought more traffic past a spot on the map that has considerable significance in Canadian history. Today, an interpretive centre and gift shop are located at the site, but in 1962 there was not much for passers-by to see at Craigellachie but the diminutive railway station and a cairn commemorating the driving of the last spike on the CPR. The photograph of Donald Smith (Lord Strathcona) bending to his work must be among the most iconic images from Canada's past.

Yet 50 years ago there was little to draw people's attention to the spot beside the highway where the historic event took place. The cairn, which had replaced an even more modest obelisk in 1927, was yet to acquire its substantial plaque-encrusted base. It was not until 1985 that the base was added as a way of marking the centennial of the great event.

Like the opening of the highway many years later, the ceremony at Craigellachie did not go entirely as planned. Governor General Lord Lansdowne intended to provide a silver spike for the occasion, but was called back to Ottawa before the ceremony took place. An ordinary iron spike was used, but apparently even this was removed soon after it was driven home and replaced with yet another spike. It was feared that the original would attract souvenir hunters.

Today, Craigellachie is worth a stop before proceeding to Sicamous. The four-lane stretch of highway beyond Malakwa has been there for a long time, as have the fruit stands that bring a reminder that here the highway runs close to the north end of the Okanagan Valley. Sicamous now bills itself as the Houseboat Capital of Canada. But the houseboat rentals that draw vacationers today were virtually unknown 50 years ago.

The cairn at Craigellachie marking the site of the 1885 completion of the Canadian Pacific Railway.

Around Sicamous, the path of the TCH has changed over the years. It was not until after the Second World War that a bridge was built across the channel that links Mara and Shuswap Lakes. The bridge stood at the foot of Main Street and replaced a ferry that ran from the bottom of what is now Finlayson Street. Traffic from the east (what there was of it) came in on what is now Maier Road, which today becomes a service road on the south side of the modern highway. Maier Road continues west of Highway 97A as Main Street—the street that led to the old bridge.

Like other towns in this part of British Columbia's interior, Sicamous was affected significantly by the opening of Rogers Pass. East-west traffic increased dramatically in the 1960s, and new gas stations and motels sprang up. Three motels that date from that era are clustered around the intersection of Main and Paradise near the centre of town. One of them, The Cedars, lives up to its name. The cedars have had a half century to grow since the rustic motel appeared on this property. They give the place the feel of being out in the country. Rumour has it that the buildings took a break from being a motel for a while, the units being converted into commercial spaces. Today, they have reverted to their original function.

Above: Sicamous, a resort town self-styled as the "houseboat capital of Canada" means "river circling mountains" in the Secwepemc or Shuswap language. Sicamous is surrounded by more than a thousand kilometres of shoreline.

Below: The Cedars Motel, located in downtown Sicamous, maintains its rustic charm.

Clark Saunders

Andybremner2012 / www.en.wikipedia.org

Peter St. John

The TCH, as well as the main line of the Canadian Pacific Railway, parallels the South Thompson River, which originates at the outlet of Little Shuswap Lake at the town of Chase. Flowing through a wide valley, it joins its northern sister in Kamloops.

Within a few years of the opening of Rogers Pass, a new route—the present one—was built along the northern edge of town. (Today it passes a miniature golf course, a reminder of a sport that was invented between the wars but increased in popularity in the postwar years.) The highway project included the construction of a new bridge. The old Bellevue Hotel was partially destroyed to make way for the new structure. After the hotel's remains had been left unoccupied for several years Gordon and Ethel Bell bought what was left, including most of the contents, and hauled it all bit by bit to their heritage town at Three Valley Gap.

Today's highway crosses the channel on the bridge that displaced the old hotel. It then carries on toward Salmon Arm. But just across the channel, signs for the Old Sicamous Road on the north side of the TCH indicate remnants of a westward route that dates back to the days of the ferry.

At the little town of Canoe the present highway turns due south on an alignment that is otherwise known as 50 Street NE. Along its east side stands an intermittent series of motels that took up their positions shortly after this route was established. It is a route that makes another sharp turn westward (at the junction with Highway 97B) as it continues to skirt Salmon Arm. Anyone interested in getting a sense of an older way through town may choose to take the appropriately named Lakeshore Road and Lakeshore Drive as they pass through the city centre. Towards the west end of town old and new routes come together as the TCH runs along 10 Avenue SW before making another decisive bend northward up the west side of the inlet of Shuswap Lake for which Salmon Arm is named.

The next stretch of highway is currently designated a "wine route"—which shows how much things have changed over the decades. Few midcentury Canadians had developed a taste for wine. In those days, the development of vineyards in these parts (like the popularity of houseboats) still lay in the future. However, some of the lakeside resorts that are a feature of this region follow a tradition that dates back almost to the coming of the railway.

On the west side of the road at Tappen, an imposing historic heritage house has stood as a landmark and centre of hospitality for more than a century. Today, it bears the facetious moniker, the Trickle Inn. Earlier generations knew it as the Carlin House.

At Carlin, Calhoun Road approaches from the left until it runs parallel to the TCH. As it runs south from here back toward Tappen it marks an earlier alignment of the highway, replaced by the present route in 1954.

Just down the road, Blind Bay attracts not only short-term tourists but also long-term retirees, as affluent and aging baby boomers swell the demand for pleasant places in which to live out their declining years. They even have a new four-lane stretch of highway to travel when they head out into the country.

After the resort town of Sorrento, bits of today's Trans-Canada still twist and turn along an old alignment that hugs the lakeshore.

The wooden wharf in Salmon Arm, British Columbia.

Straitgate / www.en.wikipedia.org

flying phil

www.kitimatmuseum.ca

Another opening, another ribbon cutting. Highways Minister Philip Gaglardi (1913-1995) oversaw the rapid expansion of B.C.'s paved road system in the 1950s and 1960s in high style. Here, Flying Phil does the honours on the Terrace to Kitimat highway in November 1957.

WITH CONSTRUCTION COSTS SHARED BETWEEN THE FEDERAL AND PROVINCIAL GOVERNMENTS, the pace at which progress was made on building the Trans-Canada Highway depended not only on the policy of the government of the day in Ottawa but on the relative wealth of each province and the political outlook of successive provincial governments. So, for instance, though the CCF government of Tommy Douglas made a push to complete Saskatchewan's portion of the No. 1 Highway by 1957 (thus becoming the first province to do so), oil-rich Alberta was able to twin much of the route long before Saskatchewan could contemplate such extravagance. In Manitoba, road construction made much less progress under the fiscally conservative leadership of Liberal-Progressive Premier Douglas Campbell (1948–1958) than it did under his successor, Progressive Conservative Duff Robin (1958–1967).

If premiers had a say in these matters, so did ministers of highways. Of all the men who occupied this position in the Western provinces during the postwar years, none could have been more colourful than Philip Gaglardi, popularly known as "Flying Phil". Appointed minister of Public Works by W.A.C. Bennett when the Social Credit came to power in 1952, Gaglardi's responsibilities included highways and bridges. Three years later, "Highways" was made a ministry of its own.

Based in Kamloops, Gaglardi was a Pentecostal pastor who, like Alberta premiers "Bible Bill" Aberhart and Ernest Manning, continued to make religious broadcasts throughout his political career. He was always happy to give God credit when the sun chose to shine on any ceremonial occasion. Gaglardi approached the work of road

A "hands-on" kind of minister, Gaglardi flew to northern B.C. in 1956 to watch the early stages of construction of Highway No. 25. It was convincing the premier to buy a Learjet for this kind of government travel that earned him his nickname, "Flying Phil." But using the jet for family travel later got him fired from the Highways portfolio.

www.kitimatmuseum.ca

and bridge building—as he approached everything else—with enthusiasm.

Canadian motorists were used to waiting while construction crews worked on a section of new highway or drizzled oil on gravel. Westbound traffic might wait 10 or 20 minutes for the approach of a pilot vehicle followed by an endless line of eastbound cars and trucks whooshing past the open windows on a hot day. In the mountains of British Columbia the wait might be accompanied by the sound of blasting. Under Gaglardi's mandate construction seemed to be happening everywhere, and the "sorry for the delay" signs led to his being nicknamed "Sorry Phil". Blame for the ubiquity of toll bridges was often laid at his door, too.

With his flamboyant style, Phil had a way of getting into the news. He sometimes played fast and loose with the niceties of financial accounting. Charges of nepotism and cronyism were often in the air. Speed limits meant

nothing to him. When he was stopped for speeding on one of his own highways, he would claim that he was just "testing the curves". But the "Flying Phil" sobriquet really owed its origins to his success in getting the premier to agree to the purchase of a Lear Jet for government use. As good as they were, highways could not always get him to his destination quickly enough to suit Phil.

On the ground, he pursued his aims with passion and boldness. He was not afraid of innovation. Hundreds of thousands of tons of sawdust were dumped in the marshlands of Burnaby as a foundation for the Trans-Canada Highway and, later, the Deas Tunnel was built near the mouth of the Fraser River where some of his advisors insisted it would be washed away. They were proved wrong.

The word "impossible" was not in Phil Gaglardi's vocabulary.

Peter St. John

This reconstructed pithouse is one of four in the Secwepmec Museum and Heritage Park in Kamloops. The park, with its excellent museum and interpretive centre, is immediately north of the TCH, just east of its junction with the Yellowhead.

At Chase, where Little Shuswap Lake empties into the South Thompson River, the older through-town route passes some heritage buildings that have been given recent attention and offers accommodations at the vintage Overlander Motel before rejoining the modern highway. From here the TCH passes through the attractive farmland of the South Thompson Valley as it makes its way to Kamloops.

Kamloops is a city that has grown prodigiously in the last half century, its exurbia stretching far to the east. The Trans-Canada's approach becomes a four-lane highway as it passes classic motels (including one actually named the "Trans-Canada") that today are almost lost among flashy car dealerships and other modern amenities. The exit to the city centre at Battle Street parallels the railway. The first business this old route passes is Jay's Service. Located at the intersection of Battle and Columbia, this period building still bears the red stars that once marked it as a Texaco gas station. Its old neighbours—a Royalite service station and a Tastee Freez—are gone now, but Jay's survived a re-routing of the highway onto Columbia Street in the early 1970s. An older alignment had taken traffic through the centre of town and nearer the river, while today's highway runs along even farther south and farther from the heart of historic Kamloops as it prepares to disgorge much of its westbound traffic onto the Coquihalla Highway.

Opposite: Peter St. John

from
KAMLOOPS
– to VANCOUVER

T hough not the oldest route through Kamloops, Columbia Street is certainly older than the modern bypass. It cuts through a predominantly residential area but also passes the Royal Inland Hospital as well as a number of motels that bear witness to the fact that this was once the preferred route through town. Eventually Columbia bends south through a modern commercial area to intersect with the present TCH.

A half dozen kilometres to the west, the Coquihalla Highway (No. 5), completed in

Chensiyuan / www.en.wikipedia.org

1986, takes Vancouver-bound motorists on a southbound shortcut to the coast. But a half century ago a traveller's best option was to continue west on what was then—and still remains—the No. 1 Highway. Though it may take longer to drive than the four-lane Coquihalla, many would argue that it is the more attractive route.

The journey begins by crossing a semi-arid landscape marked by sagebrush and irrigation sprinklers. The highway itself is a much-upgraded version of the old route. A steep climb along Kamloops Lake leads to a viewpoint and picnic spot that provide an impressive outlook over the lake to the east, while the descent on the other side offers a view of the western reaches of the same lake.

But anyone in the driver's seat is well advised to keep their eyes on the road because this is a winding stretch of highway. At the west end of the lake, the highway passes the little town of Savona. An older through-town route meanders through the strung-out community by the lake.

The Thompson River flows westward out of Kamloops Lake. The highway follows the Thompson, turning south at Cache Creek in an

Above: Kamloops, photographed from Summit Drive, just off the TCH, west of its junction with the Yellowhead Highway.

Opposite: Kamloops Lake, a widening of the Thompson River and a descendant of the glacial waters that filled the valley for thousands of years, photographed from a viewpoint just east of Savona.

Peter St. John

Travellers on the Old No. 1 West would be hard pressed to miss Ashcroft Manor, south of Cache Creek. Nor should they, for the teahouse is certainly worth a stop.

effort to keep the river in sight. Here among a few more recent chain motels can be found some veterans of the past. The aptly named Tumbleweed Motel sports fresh blue trim, while the faded glitz of the Castle Motel recalls a time when its battlements prompted children to beg their parents to stop there for the night. In the centre of town, the Oasis Hotel has been for decades the spot where the Greyhound buses stop.

Though the town of Ashcroft lies off No. 1 Highway, the Trans-Canada runs right past the door of Ashcroft Manor. At least the house, built in 1862 by the pioneer-ranching Cornwall family, was on the route until it burned down in 1943. The landmark roadhouse is still there, though, standing on the east side of the highway. Re-calling the days when miners bound for the Cariboo made a rest stop here, the place has invited travellers to pause for refreshment ever since. Today known as Ashcroft Manor Teahouse, it serves "delicious food" in a "historic atmosphere", according to a recent patron.

Its location is a reminder that a road of sorts passed its front door long before the Trans-Canada Highway was a gleam in anyone's eye. Even the railway did not come through these parts until a couple of decades after the Cornwall brothers took up residence.

The approach to Spences Bridge brings travellers past the vener-able Hilltop Gardens, the largest of the surviving fruit stands along the Thompson River. Spences Bridge itself is named for the man who built the first bridge across the Thompson here. Spences Bridge boasts two bridges. The older one crosses the river at a right angle,

southcentral british columbia

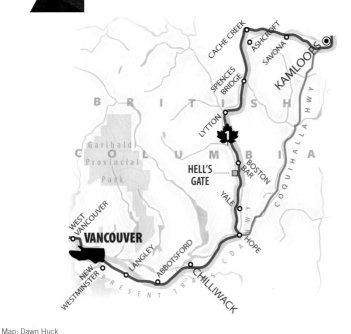

Map: Dawn Huck

Canstockphoto/CSP - 201810

ALTHOUGH THE COQUIHALLA HAS BEEN THE PREFERRED ROUTE SINCE IT WAS ADDED IN THE 1980S, THE ROUTE OF THE NO. 1 HIGHWAY IN MUCH OF B.C.'S INTERIOR IS ESSENTIALLY UNCHANGED FROM WHAT IT WAS 50 YEARS AGO. IN THE LOWER FRASER VALLEY THE PATH OF THE OLD YALE ROAD HELPED TO DETERMINE THE HIGHWAY'S ROUTE UNTIL A NEW FOUR-LANE HIGHWAY WAS CONSTRUCTED IN THE EARLY 1960S.

BRITISH COLUMBIA PROVINCIAL MINERAL

JADE OR NEPHRITE

Courtesy of Roy Carlson Collection

Jade was chosen as B.C.'s mineral emblem in 1968, but the people of British Columbia have been using it to create adzes, axes and chisels for almost 4,000 years. This is remarkable, for jade, which consists mainly of nephrite and is one of the world's hardest materials, is exceptionally difficult to work in the absence of high speed power tools and diamond drills. Today, jade is mined in many places in B.C., used to make jewellery and ornaments, including the bear, above, and exported to Asia.

Canstockphoto/CSP - 8904438

The Thompson River valley becomes a canyon near Spences Bridge.

while the structure that carries through-traffic across the river today takes a more oblique approach. Accommodations can be found in the neighbouring 60-something-year-old Baits Motel, a roadside spot with a name that must appeal to fishing enthusiasts and *Psycho* aficionados alike.

It is in the neighbourhood of Spences Bridge that the river valley becomes a canyon. The CPR and CNR each take a side of the canyon (as the first to arrive, the CP engineers got first pick). When one line crosses to the other side of the canyon (as happens in the Fraser Canyon at Siska, south of Lytton) the other has to trade places with it. And of course, since railways require more gentle grades than roads do, it is the highway that has to make the more frequent accommodations. In the stretch beyond Spences Bridge, the highway crosses the rail line several times, sometimes above it, sometimes below.

Along this stretch of highway two stopping places welcome travellers who want to enjoy a picnic or to camp overnight. Goldpan and Skihist Provincial Parks are both beautifully situated on the Thompson River. Skihist opened to the public in 1956.

It is at the old village of Lytton that the Thompson flows into the Fraser, the river that carves its canyon as it flows southward. Here the exit onto Main Street takes travellers along the old route as it wends its way through the more venerable parts of this historic town.

Courtesy of the Village of Lytton, B.C.

At Boston Bar, a bridge now crosses the canyon to the once or-phaned hamlet of North Bend. Bypassed by the highway, until 1986 the village could be accessed from the east side of the canyon only by means of an aerial cable ferry that carried one vehicle at a time. The carrier can still be seen—along with an interpretive display—at the side of the road. The building of the bridge brought North Bend's near isolation to an end. The only problem was that more people wanted to get out than get in. The bridge seems to have hastened the village's decline.

In 1950, travellers passing through Boston Bar on their way to the coast still had four hours of driving ahead of them. That's four more hours of the kids asking, "Are we there yet?" If it was late in the day, they might stop for the night at the Shady Rest Auto Camp south of town. That's what it was called in its early days, which date from around 1930. Today, it goes by the name of the Old Towne Inn, and it is still in business. Most of the other auto courts and motels from that era in these parts lie in ruins.

Above: The Thompson River joins the Fraser at Lytton.

Below: No longer used, the aerial cable ferry now serves to inform motorists, rather than carry them across the canyon.

🚗

The coming of the CPR to the Fraser and Thompson canyons in the 1880s displaced much of the 20-year-old Cariboo Road. It was not until 1926 that a Cariboo Highway opened

Clark Saunders

as a section of the Trans-Canada. Then, when new construction was undertaken beginning in the late 1950s, a series of seven new tunnels were included. These, of course, were real tunnels—not like the snow sheds of Rogers Pass—and were sure to provide excitement for baby boom travellers. Built between 1957 and 1964, they mark a period when road and tunnel construction involved a good deal of blasting, and motorists—when they were not waiting for the dust to clear or for a pilot vehicle to lead single-lane traffic heading in the opposite direction past the construction—crept along the cliff edges with the sense that they were just inches from falling into the canyon.

On the route southward, the first (and, at 610 metres, the longest) tunnel is encountered south of Boston Bar at China Bar. It is followed by brother tunnels called Ferrabee, Hell's Gate, Alexandra, Sailor Bar, Saddle Rock and Yale; the last is located just before the town that provides its name.

The tunnel that derives its handle from possibly the most famous spot in the canyon is the one named after Hell's Gate. South of Boston Bar, this narrowing of the canyon made its churning waters infamous long before rail or road passed this way. But travellers of a half century ago might not have bothered to stop here. The descending aerial tram that affords a closer look did not open for business until 1971.

As the highway approaches Spuzzum, it crosses from the east to the west side of the Fraser. The present bridge is the grandchild of the one built a kilometre or two to the north in 1863 as part of the Cariboo Road. After the first Alexandra Bridge was destroyed by flood in the 1890s, a generation would pass before a new suspension bridge was built in 1926. Using the footings of the old bridge and with a deck that was three metres higher than the old one (the flood had taught its lesson), its construction was part of the building of the Cariboo Highway. When the present bridge was opened in 1964, the old familiar—and, by today's standards, narrow—landmark was closed to vehicular traffic.

However, the second Alexandra Bridge can still be reached on foot by a trail leading from the eponymous provincial park. The trail is a vestigial remnant of the old

Hell's Gate. Few midcentury travellers got to see it.

BC Archives / A-03882 / C 1914

Both photos: Clark Saunders

highway that used to carry traffic to it. On the east bank and north of the park, the crumbling building that used to welcome guests under the name of "Alexandra Lodge" serves as a reminder that this has been a stopping place through the years of the bridge's various incarnations.

At Spuzzum, little of a commercial nature remains from the 20th century. A general store and an Esso station are gone, but on a section of old highway an older store—converted into a home with a bed of flowers taking the spot where gas pumps used to stand—survived into the present century. Across the road (and visible from the present highway) another residence enjoyed an earlier existence as the Spuzzum Hotel. Japanese Canadians took up residence here after the Second World War. Released from the interment camps to which they had been sent in wartime, they were still not allowed to return to the coast. Some ended up staying on into the postwar era.

Travellers wanting to get an impression of the auto court of bygone days may want to glance in the direction of the moss-covered cabins of the Colonial Inn Motel near Spuzzum, while at Yale, the old Golden Nugget Motel can barely announce its presence. When last sighted, the remaining letters in its sign spelled, "Gol Nu get Mote."

Yale—the historic head of navigation on the Fraser—is the last

Top: the Old Alexandra Bridge over the Fraser Canyon is now used only by pedestrians and, perhaps, cyclists.

Above: Alexandra Lodge sits, waiting for time to spell its end.

Peter St. John

The Fraser River upstream from Yale. The granite ridge across the water protected an ancient Aboriginal encampment.

community before Hope. But about five kilometres before the Trans-Canada reaches the town that marks a convergence of highways, the road passes the Lake of the Woods Motel. With units set near the edge of a small lake, this modest resort has faded somewhat since the 1960s when visitors enjoyed setting out from shore in rowboats.

Just before the No. 1 bends eastward to cross the Fraser on its final approach to Hope, a junction with the No. 7 Highway offers an alternate route into the big city. Known as the Lougheed Highway this road was commissioned in 1941 with construction beginning at the Vancouver end of its route. Through the 1950s and '60s it progressed in stages and with occasional realignments, finally reaching this junction in 1973.

Hope also marks the western terminus of the No. 3 (or Crowsnest) Highway, which stretches across much of British Columbia and Alberta. It rejoins the No. 1 at Medicine Hat, its eastern terminus. The most recent addition to this embarrassment of options is the Coquihalla, which heads northward until it is reunited with the No. 1 west of Kamloops. Bearing the number "5", this highway superseded an older route (presently doing business under the name "5A") that, like the present four-lane, ran through Merritt but, unlike the Coquihalla, finds its southern end at Princeton.

The town of Hope itself lies east of the bridge that takes the Trans-Canada back to the left bank of the Fraser. The town centre is mostly on the east side of the highway; with its older motels and stands of evergreens, it seems to have changed very little over the decades. Certainly the route of the No. 1 Highway through town provides the modern visitor with a slight sense of time warp.

A similar sensation awaits those who, on heading west from town, watch for Flood Hope Road at Exit 168. Beginning about two kilometres west of Hope, this road is a section of old highway. The old Thunder Bird Motel with its single and duplex cabins, the Wild Rose Campground and J's Café (the last located just before the road rejoins the modern highway) all speak of an earlier era.

With the river and the railway running parallel on the right and the mountains cozying in on the left, the route over the next several kilometres has had little room for variation over the years.

Among those mountains to the south, a previously little-known peak called Slesse Mountain made the headlines on December 9,

1956, when it was the scene of what at the time was the worst disaster in Canadian aviation history. A Trans-Canada Airlines (TCA) flight crashed into the mountain killing all 62 passengers on board including five professional football players, four of them members of the Saskatchewan Roughriders.

It is a safe bet that any road including the name "Yale" marks a route dating from the 1860s that led east and north from New Westminster to the town of Yale in the Fraser Canyon. It was also the natural route to choose when highways first forged their way through this part of the country. Yale Road East follows the route of the old Trans-Canada east of Chilliwack. For the westbound traveller, one of the first opportunities to access it is found by exiting onto the Agassiz-Rosedale Highway (No. 9). Yale Road East crosses this highway almost immediately to the north of the No. 1. Passing through bucolic countryside, this two-lane route served as the Trans-Canada until about 1960. It was then that Chilliwack was bypassed by a new alignment (part of what became a four-lane freeway designated initially as "the 401") extending east to Bridal Veil Falls.

Yale Road East became British Columbia Highway 1, prior to being designated "Trans-Canada Parallel Route" by the City of Chilliwack in 2005. It provides a pleasant alternative to the modern four-lane. In fact, a modern motorist who chooses it may have the sensa-

Jonhall / www.en.wikipedia.org

Above: Rocks gathered around a propeller atop Mount Slesse near Chilliwack create a cairn that marks the site where TCA 810 met its end.

Below: It's unlikely that any of the many falls by the same name deserve it more than B.C.'s Bridal Veil Falls, for the spray is truly reminiscent of a gauzy veil.

Stephen Edwards / www.en.wikipedia.org

tion of travelling through farmland that is in danger of disappearing in the face of ever-expanding urban sprawl.

In the early postwar decades, Chilliwack itself had a fraction of its current population of 80,000. But then, as now, the intersection known as Five Corners marked the spot where Yale Road East crosses Young Road and becomes Yale Road West. The fifth corner belongs to Wellington Avenue, which heads off from the same intersection in a northwesterly direction. Just a block along Wellington (at the corner of Main Street) stands the Royal Hotel, a landmark hostelry dating from 1908. For nearly 70 years (from 1926 to 1995) it was owned and operated by the Berrys, father and son. Berry *fils*—known as Buck—always left a big impression, being big of bulk and big of personality. Since leaving the management of the Berry family, the hotel has been undergoing renovations. Efforts are being made to retain the period character of the place, while vintage photographs on the walls recall the accommodations—and the watering hole—of yesteryear.

From Five Corners, the old route (Yale Road West) wends its way south through the centre of Chilliwack before bending westward as it approaches the modern highway. Leaving the city it becomes in effect a frontage road, running parallel to the present Trans-Canada along the four-lane highway's north side. The frontage road is interrupted by a canal, beyond which it becomes Parallel Road North.

From here, until it begins to bypass the burgeoning city of Abbotsford, the path of the modern Trans-Canada approximates the route it travelled in the 1950s. But on the modern highway's approach to Abbotsford an opportunity presents itself to follow some of the old route through town. Taking Exit 95 and driving north a couple of blocks on Whatcom Road, drivers can turn left and enter Abbotsford on Old Yale Road. Although for much of its route it looks

Chilliwack in the days when Old Highway No. 1 went through town.

chilliwack.pastperfect-online.com/33335cgi

Photo Credit: Chilliwack Museum & Arc

Elmer G. Weins / Courtesy of www.yarrowbc.ca

like any suburban drive, its name commemorates the oldest road through the Fraser Valley. When its four lanes are reduced to two for a section west of Eagle Mountain Drive, it takes on something of its midcentury appearance.

There are a couple of name changes after the road crosses Highway 11, as it becomes first Essendene Avenue and then South Fraser Way. Clearbrook—the west-side suburb through which the route passes—was a separate community before Abbotsford mushroomed to absorb it. At Parkview, where South Fraser Way bends to the left, the old route goes straight ahead on another iteration of Old Yale Road. After meeting Maclure Road at a T-junction, the old route makes a left turn and crosses the modern Trans-Canada at a major interchange. From this point the old route takes on the name, Fraser Highway. Both those who have stayed on the modern highway and those who have followed the old route through Abbotsford may want to travel an extended section of the Fraser Highway as it runs west-by-northwestward roughly parallel to the No. 1 and a few kilometres south of it.

What is initially a two-lane highway passes stretches of trees and bush that conceal whatever changes the past half century has brought and creates an effect of being transported back in time. Although the proportion of built-up areas has grown over that period, there are still garden centres here and there along the route to remind travellers that this is a part of the country where produce continues to be grown.

Travellers on today's Trans-Canada Highway might find it hard to visualize travelling conditions encountered by earlier generations.

The blacksmith's shop
at Fort Langley NHS.

Peter St. John

The first town to be encountered on the Fraser Highway is Alder-grove. Here, the tree-lined town centre retains some of its old character. To the west, at 260th Street, the Twilight Drive-In theatre maintains an old tradition as it sports a sign advertising shows that begin "Daily at Dusk". Today revenues are supplemented by weekly swap meets on Sundays.

To the left, at varying distances from the Fraser Highway, the Old Yale Road appears and disappears from time to time between Aldergrove and Surrey. The Fraser Highway itself becomes a four-lane affair as it approaches Langley, another town that has expanded dramatically since the middle of the last century. In the city centre westbound traffic comes to an intersection at 206th Street where it is confronted by two blocks of one-way traffic coming in the oppos-ite direction. The best option is to take a right on 206th Street, turn left on to 56th Avenue, and left again at Glover Road to get onto the onward route.

However, travellers should consider making a right turn at Glover Road (a.k.a. Route 10) and following it to the charming town of Fort Langley on the Fraser River. The town and the restored fur-trading fort for which it is named have never been on the Trans-Canada Highway, though they are closer to the four-lane highway created in the early 1960s than they are to the old road. However, since 1958, when British Columbia celebrated the centenary of the creation of the mainland colony of that name, the fort has been a popular stopping place for families on holiday.

In 1858, in a measure designed to assert British authority in a territory that had seen the chaotic influx of adventurers in search of gold, the mainland of British Columbia was established as a colony at a ceremony at Fort Langley. Although the Canadian government recognized the historic significance of the fort as far back as 1923, it was only in 1931 that the one remaining original building was opened to the public. But it was the centenary of 1958 (the first in a series of celebrations that kept B.C. celebrating the centennials of various stages in its development through 1966-1967 and 1971) that prompted a concerted effort to rebuild the old post. By the end of 1958, two buildings, including the big house, were ready to receive visitors. Easy access from the TCH has helped to draw them in ever since.

Back at the larger centre of Langley itself, the Fraser Highway continues west, crossing a bypass that didn't exist in the days of midcentury travel. However, the Westward Inn Motel on the south side of the highway just beyond the bypass has offered accommodation since the days when transcontinental travellers were more likely to pass its door.

As it enters the growing Vancouver suburb of Surrey, the old highway passes through some green reserves that mercifully have been saved from destruction. Having run as straight as an arrow for many kilometres, the Fraser Highway comes up against King George Boulevard and runs north on it. Formerly known as the King George Highway (named for George VI) and bearing the number "99", from 1940 until the end of the 1950s, this was the main route south from Vancouver to the United States. But running north from the point where the Fraser Highway joins it, Highway 99 and the TCH ran together as far as New Westminster.

Along the way the street passes through a commercial district before bending west and descending a long hill to the aged Pattullo Bridge. Named after a premier of British Columbia, the bridge, completed in 1937, carries traffic across the Fraser River.

The late 1930s marked the construction of a number of iconic bridges on the west coast of North America. Notwithstanding that the Great Depression had devastated the economy (or because of it, given that some of these constructions were government projects), the Golden Gate Bridge, the San Francisco-Oakland Bay Bridge, and the Lion's Gate Bridge were all undertaken during the same period. The Pattullo Bridge's distinctive "through arch" design may be reminiscent of the Sydney Harbour Bridge (its elder by five years) and is echoed by the

Named for Dufferin (or Duff) Pattullo, B.C. premier from 1933 to 1941, Pattullo Bridge was almost futuristic in its design when it was opened in 1937.

DennisSylvesterHurd / www.en.wikipedia.org

Ron B. Thomson / www.en.wikipedia.org

On June 17, 1958, the crane perched on a north-side span reaching out over the inlet proved too heavy for the uncompleted structure supporting it. It collapsed, taking 79 workers with it. Of these, 18 were killed. A diver searching for bodies was later added to the death toll. It was one of the worst bridge disasters in Canadian history.

The bridge was finally completed in 1960, but those who lost their lives were not forgotten. The tragedy was commemorated in song and story. As early as 1962, country singer Jimmy Dean (later to add to his fame through sausage manufacturing) came out with a truly awful song called, "Steel Men". Its shortcomings begin (but do not end) with the jauntiness of the tune—and this just four years after all these men had lost their lives. Ten years later Stompin' Tom Connors did slightly better with his narrative song, "The Bridge Came Tumbling Down". At the bridge itself, the dead were remembered with a plaque.

A more worthy memorial came in 1994 when those who died in the collapse, as well as four others who were killed during the bridge's construction, were recognized with its official renaming as the Ironworkers Memorial Second Narrows Crossing.

And what about the railway? Some mistakenly think that the bridge to the east of the road bridge is the old structure of 1925. But it is not. Trains stopped using the old, formerly dual-purpose bridge in 1968 when it was replaced by the structure you see today. The old bridge and its cement piers were removed two years later.

I N THE POSTWAR YEARS, BRITISH COLUMBIANS SOME-TIMES RESENTED THE TOLLS they had to pay to cross the many bridges they encountered to get from point A to point B. The justification for the tolls, of course, was that these bridges were costly to build. But one was costly not just in money but in human lives.

Contrary to what some might expect, it is not the Lion's Gate (or First Narrows) Bridge that carries the Trans-Canada Highway across Burrard Inlet to Greater Vancouver's North Shore. The TCH takes the bridge at the Second Narrows. For 15 years after the end of World War II, vehicles continued to share with trains a combined road and railway bridge. Used by vehicles as soon as it was completed in 1925, train traffic was added the following year.

Long before the 1950s, this low bridge had become a problem. Although a lift had been added to the original design, whenever it was raised to allow ships to pass, both train and vehicular traffic ground to a halt. In 1955, the decision was made to construct a lofty six-lane steel-truss cantilever bridge to transport vehicles, while leaving the old bridge to train traffic.

Above: Ironworkers Memorial Second Narrows Crossing

Canstockphoto / CSP - 12477810

larger arch of the first Port Mann Bridge, the longest bridge on the Trans-Canada Highway. Opened in 1964 as part of the newer TCH (numbered "401" at that time), the Port Mann Bridge was positioned upstream and around a bend of the river from the Pattullo. Although the Pattullo Bridge is a generation older, it carries on (for now, at least), while in 2012 its 48-year-old cousin was replaced by a bold, expensive, and not entirely satisfactory new structure. Shortly after it was opened, ice forming on its cables and falling on vehicles below indicated that some problems still needed to be resolved.

The Lion's Gate Bridge at nightfall. A contemporary of the Pattullo Bridge, some are surprised to find it's not on the Trans-Canada Highway.

On the farther shore of the Fraser, the Pattullo Bridge deposits its traffic in the historic city of New Westminster. When it comes to choosing a route for the onward journey, options abound. Staying with the flow of traffic as it leads northwestward onto McBride Boulevard was and remains the choice favoured by many who are headed, via 10th Avenue and Kingsway (at various times designated as Highways 99A and 1A), for Vancouver. This is the route that eventually leads across the Lion's Gate Bridge to the north shore.

But an alternative can be found by taking the right-hand exit shortly after crossing the bridge and driving onto McBride southbound as it leads to both Royal Avenue and, farther down the hill, Columbia Street. Columbia looks to a past when it was New Westminster's thriving main drag. Business suffered after 1964 when the new TCH freeway not only took transnational traffic away from New Westminster but conveyed regional shoppers from Surrey and Burnaby more easily to the bigger rival city of Vancouver.

Both Royal and Columbia run in a southwesterly direction. Turning right from either of them onto 8th Street will put travellers onto the old Trans-Canada route. At 10th Avenue traffic crosses from New Westminster into Burnaby. Here, in the days of the old highway, 8th Street became Douglas Road. Today, a long section of Douglas Road—starting at 10th Avenue—goes under the moniker "Canada Way". At Sprott Street, where Canada Way bends westward, the old route continues north on what is still called Douglas Road. It may be hard to believe that this modest drive, paling as it does into insignificance compared to the many more major routes in this part of the metropolis, was once the Trans-Canada Highway.

Drawing little attention to itself, Douglas Road crosses the modern TCH, curves west and blends onto the Lougheed Highway, disappearing for a short while as a separate entity. But if motorists, after passing Brentwood Town Centre mall and crossing Willingdon Avenue, will kindly watch for Madison Street a half-kilometer farther on, a right turn at this point will lead almost immediately to a continuation of Douglas Road. Passing the Masonic Cemetery, it runs northwest until it intersects with Boundary Road, the street that marks the divide between Burnaby and Vancouver. This distinctive street is marked—as it has been for many decades—by a wide central boulevard down which march a line of tall metal hydro pylons.

It is best now to get over to the modern highway as it approaches what some remember as the Second Narrows Bridge. The present TCH freeway is reached by turning west (into the City of Vancouver) on East Hastings Street and then north on the Cassiar Connector, an access road that blends onto the new highway. On the west side of the highway is the site of the annual Pacific National Exhibition, a fair that dates back more than a century. Boomer kids who headed to the PNE to enjoy its attractions were thrilled when, in 1958, a permanent wooden roller coaster was added to the rides that came and went with the exhibition. It is still there, anchoring the Playland Amusement Park. Another structure that made its appearance in the neighbourhood in the postwar era was the Empire Stadium. Built in 1954 for the British Empire and Commonwealth Games of that year, it served as the home of the BC Lions until it was demolished in 1993. The longer-lived Vancouver Forum has had a more impressive run. Since 1931 it has been a venue for events as varied as hockey games and rock concerts.

The kilometres travelled by the Trans-Canada in Vancouver proper are few but full of things to catch the eye. Within minutes of entering this northeast corner of the city, however, vehicles leave it by way of the Iron Workers Memorial Second Narrows Crossing.

Opposite: Canstockphoto / CSP - 8216775

from VANCOUVER to - VICTORIA

West Vancouver Archives / The Coast Publishing Co. Ltd. / 3609.WVA.PHO

Opposite: Canstockphoto / CSP- 8216775

Known when it was completed as the Second Narrows Bridge, the Iron Workers Memorial Second Narrows Crossing has deposited northbound TCH traffic on the north shore of Burrard Inlet since the bridge was opened in 1960. As with the Pattullo Bridge, a number of options are available on the farther shore. Today the principal route (the No. 1) goes straight on before bending to the left and climbing the long incline of the Upper Levels Highway. Beginning with a two-lane rendition built in the late 1950s, it was the West Vancouver section of this road that was constructed first, with the portion carrying traffic through the City and District of North Vancouver taking shape shortly afterwards. But closer to the water, the older route can still be followed, with a couple of options available. Both begin by leaving the present highway by a cloverleaf at the north end of the bridge and taking Main Street westbound.

Once the lower route became available, heavier vehicles stayed on Main Street as it became Cotton Drive and split into 3rd Street East and Low Level Road (other options). But cars could—and still can—follow an older route, turning north on Mountain Highway. As it approaches the Upper Levels Highway, this road makes a sharp left turn and becomes Keith Road as it crosses Lynn Creek on an old, narrow, green truss bridge. Keith Road passes older houses (pre- and post-Second World War) mixed with newer replacements. After making a bend it acquires a wide central boulevard before widening again to pass lovely Victoria Park. Drivers who simply want to get on with it can continue west when this road links up with 13th Street.

But to get a taste of the commercial heart of North Vancouver,

VANCOUVER, B.C., CANADA
North Shore Marine Drive at Garrow Bay

Above: Looking westward toward Garrow Bay and Bowen Island, this late 1940s postcard shows Marine Drive winding around the West Vancouver shore with tiny Eagle Island just offshore.

Opposite: Nanaimo Harbour. This is the view travellers on the TCH see as they arrive on Vancouver Island.

The Tomahawk Restaurant dates from 1926.

www.tomahawkrestaurant.com

motorists may want to drive downhill to the other old route, 3rd Street. This can be done at a number of points. One option is to take Lonsdale Avenue, the street that divides crossing streets into their "east" and "west" designations. Down at the water, Lonsdale Quay is a commercial and entertainment hub that transformed this area in the 1980s. In the first two postwar decades few could have foreseen that the waterfront here would become a tourist destination.

Although there are a number of ways to cross much of North Vancouver from east to west, all but the Upper Levels Highway come together eventually to form Marine Drive. South of this thoroughfare, on Philip Avenue at 15th Street, stands the iconic Tomahawk Restaurant. Begun in 1926 on a site on Marine Drive, the Tomahawk moved to its present location in 1960. Touted as greater Vancouver's first drive-in restaurant, it has always been a family business, having been started by Chick Chamberlain and now being run by his son, Chuck. Fourteen original stools have been recovered and do duty at the counter. The architecture of the present building, with its pitched roof (reminiscent of a First Nations longhouse) and its stone and timber construction, speaks of the period in which it was erected. The Aboriginal decorations are a link with the past as well, although today's menu brings things up to date by including both traditional and more innovative items.

A few blocks west on Marine Drive, Capilano Road provides access to a number of uphill attractions. The Grouse Mountain aerial tramway did not appear until 1966, although the history of chairlifts in the area dates back beyond the 1950s. But it is the Capilano Suspension Bridge that stands out as the undoubted granddaddy of tourist destinations in the neighbourhood. Its first incarnation flung itself across the canyon before the turn of the 20th century, but it was completely rebuilt in 1956. Further development of the property—with added features to keep the place current and competitive—has taken place in more recent years.

Capilano Suspension Bridge

Canstockphoto/CSP - 16999466

Down at the foot of Capilano Road, on the north side of Marine Drive between Capilano and the approach to the Lion's Gate Bridge, the Grouse Inn and a Travelodge are the modern successors to the motels that occupied this prime tourist property in the early postwar years.

West of the Capilano River, Marine Drive brings motorists into

southwestern british columbia

Map: Dawn Huck

SINCE THE LATE 1950S, DRIVERS WHO WANT TO MAKE TIME HAVE CHOSEN THE NORTH SHORE'S UPPER LEVELS HIGHWAY ON THE MAINLAND. ON VANCOUVER ISLAND THE HIGHWAY'S PATH HAS CHANGED IN PLACES, BUT EVEN THE MODERN ROUTE AVERAGES MORE TRAFFIC LIGHTS PER KILOMETRE THAN ANY OTHER SECTION OF THE ENTIRE TCH.

BRITISH COLUMBIA PROVINCIAL TREE

WESTERN REDCEDAR

Peter St. John

Potentially a very large tree, *Thuja plicata,* the western or Pacific redcedar, is an evergreen coniferous member of the cypress family. Native to western North America, it can be very large, ranging up to 100 metres (or 320 feet). Exceptionally long-lived, individual trees can live more than 1,000 years, with the oldest verified tree being 1,460 years.

Crucial to many West Coast cultures, which used its bark for clothing, hats, mats and baskets, its timber for houses, totem poles, canoes and masks, and its branches for fish traps, the western redcedar has often been call the "tree of life".

Peter St. John

getting to the island

IN THE FIRST TWO DECADES AFTER THE SECOND WORLD war, the experience of getting from the Canadian mainland to Vancouver Island underwent a series of major changes.

A motorist wanting to cross to the island in the late 1940s (without going through the US) had little option but to take one of the Canadian Pacific steamships from Vancouver to Victoria. Using a fleet of ships that were not well designed for the loading and unloading of vehicles, the voyage from one downtown to the other took more than six hours to complete.

When the state of Washington went into the ferry business in 1948 and bought most of the Black Ball Line's vessels as part of its new venture, company owner Captain Alexander Peabody did not have far to look in his search for a new business opportunity. Competing with CP in British Columbia would be a piece of cake. He transferred the remainder of his Black Ball fleet to B.C.'s Lower Mainland. After building ferry terminals at the sleepy fishing village of Horseshoe Bay on the mainland and at Departure Bay near Nanaimo on Vancouver Island, he assigned the venerable *Kahloke* (built in 1903) and the sleek, nearly new *Chinook II* to the Strait of Georgia run.

These were drive-on, drive-off vehicles that shortened the sailing time to the island drastically. In the ferry business, CP's days were numbered.

But although it could not have been foreseen when the new competition arrived in 1951, Black Ball's moment in the sun would be brief as well. The next year W.A.C. Bennett brought Social Credit to power in B.C. When labour unrest threatened to disrupt ferry service to the island in the late 1950s, Premier Bennett decided that the possible disruption to the province's transportation and damage to its economy could not be tolerated. Like Washington State before it, British Columbia would run its own ferry service. Highways Minister Phil Gaglardi was put in charge of making it happen. New terminals were built at Tsawwassen south of Vancouver and at Swartz Bay north of Victoria. In a hurry to find a suitable design for its own ships, two new vessels were commissioned along the lines of the new American ferry, MV *Coho*. (If you want to get an idea of what the first new B.C. ferries looked like, check out the *Coho*. It still makes the Victoria–Port Angeles trip all these years later.) The first new ships were ready to start the Tsawwassen–Swartz Bay run in 1960.

As part of the new order, the government took over Black Ball's vessels and terminals. In the ferry-building frenzy of the early 1960s, new ships eventually came on line to take over the more northerly crossing on the Trans-Canada route. The *Kahloke* and the *Chinook* were repainted in the blue and white colours of the province's "Dogwood Fleet" and were soon assigned to other duties. But although Tsawwassen has become the larger port of embarkation, Horseshoe Bay to Departure Bay continues to be the route of the Trans-Canada Highway.

the Municipality of West Vancouver. Now known as one of the most affluent communities in the country, the early postwar decades saw the district begin to transition from a sleepy, unpretentious and rather remote suburb of the big city into the place to be. Those years saw the expansion of Taylor Way leading up to the high-end British Pacific Properties and to the West Van section of the Upper Levels Highway. On its completion, the Upper Levels became the preferred Trans-Canada route to Horseshoe Bay.

Another early step toward the transformation of West Vancouver was the construction of the Park Royal Shopping Centre. Opened in 1950, it was one of the earliest projects of its kind in Canada. Small by today's standards, it was confined originally to the north side of Marine Drive and lacked the covered-over style of later malls—a style, which, of course, caught up with Park Royal itself over the years.

Across Marine Drive at the foot of Taylor Way there still stands a White Spot restaurant. This location of a west-coast chain began life as a drive-in. In the 1950s, your order would be brought to your car on long, skinny trays that extended from one window to the other.

West Vancouver was, and to some extent still is, a string of neighbourhoods stretching along the western reaches of Burrard Inlet's north shore. Ambleside borders the business district known locally as "the village". Then, along Marine Drive, there are such communities as Dundarave, West Bay, and Caulfeild [sic]. Given the price of land in this suburb, a surprising number of relatively modest homes and commercial buildings have survived from the postwar years, albeit often in different guises.

Just past West Bay, Marine Drive comes close to the water at a spot formerly known as "Suicide Bend". This dangerous bit of road has been straightened out somewhat, rebuilt with curbing, and set at a safer distance from the drink than it was when a poorly controlled vehicle might be inclined to leave the pavement at this point.

En route to Horseshoe Bay, the old highway (Marine Drive) passes the West Vancouver Yacht Club at Fisherman's Cove where, as in years gone by, some of the community's high-priced citizens park their pleasure craft.

The approaches to Horseshoe Bay village and to the ferry terminal have been reconfig-

The TCH transformed Horseshoe Bay from a fishing village to a ferry port.

Peter St. John

ured repeatedly since the 1950s. Traffic circles on the low road are just the latest subterfuges designed to confuse the unwary motorist. Drivers on the Upper Levels Highway may find it counterintuitive to bear to the right to get in line for the ferry to Vancouver Island, but that is what they must do.

The long and winding road that is Marine Drive suggests a leisurely driving pace, but "leisurely" did not generally describe the pace of a driver of the 1950s with a ferry to catch. One of the reasons for building the Upper Levels Highway was to get vehicles to the ferry in a fraction of the time it would take them to travel the lower road. A bonus is the bird's-eye view that the higher road provides of the areas through which the lower road passes.

The village of Horseshoe Bay itself has acquired a look that is decidedly up-market compared to that of the fishing port that first greeted the Black Ball ferries after the Second World War.

The Horseshoe Bay Motel, located in the heart of town, has had a makeover or two since it opened in 1961. It has always been a two-storey affair, but its colour palette is much more muted (and more in keeping with that of its present neighbours) than it was when a splash of brighter hues announced its presence in its early days.

Although the ferry terminals at both ends of the Georgia Strait crossing have expanded considerably over the past half century, they are still located at the same ports: Horseshoe Bay on the mainland and Departure Bay near Nanaimo on Vancouver Island. The crossing is a little faster now, but the route still begins with a sharp left turn out of Horseshoe Bay before the ferry heads out into open water, passing Bowen Island on the starboard side as it does so. As it approaches "the big island", it passes to the right of both Gabriola Island and the smaller Newcastle Island near the shore.

Vehicles driving off the ferry will find themselves on the TCH as it runs south on Stewart Avenue bound for downtown Nanaimo. Just before crossing the Millstone River on its final approach to the city centre, Stewart merges with the Island Highway (here also known as Terminal Avenue) coming in on the right from "up-island" regions. From this point southeastward, the Island Highway and the Trans-Canada Highway occupy much of the same pavement.

In the heart of the city, a left turn off the highway and onto Bastion Street leads to Front Street

Because of its high visibility from land and sea, the Nanimo Bastion has been called the city's premier landmark.

Ken Walker / www.en.wikipedia.org

and the venerable Nanaimo Bastion, an octagonal wooden fort built in the 1850s to defend local coal mining operations. The bastion attracted tourists young and old who came to call a century later and continues to do so a half century and more after that. Today's visitors will find it moved slightly since the 1950s. This was done in 1979, and the tower was given a major overhaul more recently still.

On its way through the centre of town the highway bends left and then right before taking a straight trajectory on its southerly exit from the city. A few blocks after it straightens out, Milton Street crosses its path. A left turn here leads in a few blocks to Esplanade where, less than a block to the north (another left turn) the last of the area's six auto courts—the Evergreen—continued to offer accommodations to holiday makers long after its midcentury heyday.

Petroglyph Provincial Park was once considered to be out in the country, but hardly seems so these days. The day park continues to provide access, by means of a short walk from the parking lot, to thousand-year-old symbolic etchings left by ancestors of First Nations people in the area.

Motorists know they are truly out of the city when they cross the Nanaimo River on a green rainbow-arched bridge. But the route from here to the beginning of the Malahat Drive is much more built up today than it was in the mid-20th century. Frequent traffic-light-controlled intersections ensure that any tendency on the part of a driver to gather speed will be shortly curtailed.

Peter St. John

Today, concrete replicas of the original images in Petroglyph Park not only allow a clearer view, but also permit interested visitors to make rubbings or tracings.

After passing the former coal-mining hamlet of Cassidy—it was mined out by 1953—the highway passes the more substantial hillside community of Ladysmith. Named for the South African town that had recently hit the headlines in the Boer War, this resource town sprang up almost overnight around the turn of the 20th century. A half century later it seemed a rather dreary place, but by the time it celebrated its centenary it was taking advantage of the impressive number of heritage buildings that dated back to its early days. Many of these can be seen—refurbished and filled with restaurants and shops that cater to the tourist trade—on First Avenue. But since 1954, the TCH has skirted the town, running along its northeast side at the foot of the hill on a road known locally as Esplanade Avenue. Buildings are found on the southwest side of this route, while the venerable Esquimalt and Nanaimo Railway runs along the side opposite.

While Ladysmith can still be seen in a motorist's rearview mirror, there is an opportunity to leave the Island Highway (the modern TCH) and venture onto Highway 1A, a stretch of old road that immediately crosses the E&N line before turning southeastward on a path that winds pleasantly along a two-lane highway with speed limits ranging from 30 to 60 kilometres an hour. This was the main route until 1950. At first the road passes near the water, then it heads farther inland, running through the woods. Just before making this transition (in the district known as Saltair), the road crosses the mouth of a tidal creek and passes the oceanfront Seaview Marine Resort. Now under the auspices of Rob and Heather Parker, the five cabins have undergone significant refurbishment in recent years and cater, as they always have, to one-night and longer-term stays. The preferred method of booking has changed, however. A brochure from the 1950s invites customers to "write, wire or phone". Talk of email, Internet and Wi-Fi would have sounded like a foreign language in those days. The salmon and trout fishing touted in the brochure is not a feature of today's website, nor is there any mention of the absence of mosquitoes—a boast made in the old flyer, suggesting that it was aimed at folks from the prairies.

Not far beyond the resort, a section of Old Victoria Road branches off to the right only to rejoin the old highway three kilometres or so farther on. Just as variations of the name "Yale Road" indicate the path of a very old route through the Lower Fraser Valley on the mainland, routes called Victoria Road and Old Victoria Road appear and disappear between Nanaimo and the Cowichan Valley, indicating a route that predates the TCH.

The most prominent town on this loop of the old highway is Chemainus. No more attractive than Ladysmith a half century ago, this former mill town now outdoes its northwesterly neighbour for

Chemainus has made its mark as a tourist destination with its array of impressive murals.

Peter St. John

Jack Most / themostinphotograpy.com

charm and quaintness. The story of its transformation did not begin until the early 1980s when, caught in a widespread recession and faced with the closure of the sawmill, the community decided to reinvent itself. Nowadays, murals on the sides of buildings can be found in many small towns across the country, but when Chemainus invited well-known artists to cover its outer walls with their works, it was a novel idea and one carried out on an impressive scale.

Over time, attractive shops and a dinner theatre were added to the list of features that have made this a tourist destination. But, of course, when the main highway passed through this place in the early postwar decades, Chemainus looked nothing like it does today. On the other hand, it has assuredly not turned into the ghost town that many—30 years ago—predicted.

Less than four kilometres south of town, the 1A Highway (a.k.a. Chemainus Road) bends to cross an old, narrow, timber truss bridge that was closed for reconstruction in 2013. When it is possible to reach the far side, drivers who intend to stay on the old highway should ignore the signs to Crofton and follow Chemainus Road as it becomes Westholme Road and passes through the Halalt First Nation. A right turn on Mount Sicker Road (not marked as such but indicated by a direction sign to the TCH half a kilometer away) soon brings this section of Highway IA back to the modern route, i.e., the Island Highway.

There has never been a time that the main route has not passed close to the heart of Duncan, the Cowichan Valley's largest town.

In the early and mid-20th century, the Cowichan Valley and its people, the Quw'utsun, gave their name to beautiful hand-knit sweaters. Today, the valley is becoming known for its vinyards and its wines.

Jack Most / themostinphotograpy.com

The units at Malahat Bungalows Motel, built in the 1940s, were given a new lease on life in the 21st century.

The world's largest hockey stick decorating the side of the Cowichan Community Centre dates back only to 1985, but one of the two landmark silver bridges that cross the Cowichan River—the smaller of the two and the one that carries Victoria-bound traffic—was built in 1949. In those days this was a two-lane highway. It was not until 1976, when the route became four-lane, that the bridge now carrying northbound traffic was added.

About five kilometres south of Duncan, Blacky's Auto Recycling has been in business since 1960. Known at one time for its impressive collection of hubcaps—numbering 10,000 at one point—developments in wheel rim technology have reduced the inventory to mere hundreds.

After the stop-and-go of many controlled intersections the Island Highway passes Mill Bay and finally begins its ascent of the Malahat Drive (named for the First Nation of the area), a stretch of highway that hugs the mountain towering over Saanich Inlet. Now a twenty-five-kilometre portion of the Trans-Canada Highway, the original road was a challenge to build in 1911. It is still a challenge to drive, especially at night. When the sun shines, though, it deserves its reputation for impressive scenery.

Although the route has been altered little over the years, some features along the way have changed. A popular rustic stopping place replete with totem poles, the Malahat Chalet was a landmark of the 1950s and '60s, but is now the site of the Malahat Drive Highway Rest Area. (As a step toward making this accident-prone road a little safer, neither this rest area nor the viewpoints on the east side of the highway are accessible to southbound traffic.) On the southward descent, the Malahat Bungalows Motel dates back to the 1940s. Since changing hands in 2010, the cabins sport a fresh and charming look.

For nearly six decades, Goldstream Provincial Park has marked the foot of the Malahat and the beginning of the final approach to Victoria. In 1956, the City of Victoria, despite claims of the local First Nations people that they had never surrendered this land, conveyed it to the provincial government for development as a provincial park. The sights of towering old growth forest, bald eagles, and salmon on their annual run have continued to make this a popular place to visit through the years.

At about the same time that Goldstream was being set up as a provincial park, the present route of the TCH was being constructed leading into Victoria. In the early days of this new route, motorists drove into the city through a different kind of forest than they encountered in the provincial park; the residential suburbs were marked by a forest of television aerials. By means of these rather unsightly rooftop devices viewers could pick up channels from Vancouver, Bellingham, Seattle and Tacoma—an embarrassment of options available to few Canadians in the early days of TV broadcasting.

Winter along the Goldstream River, with Mount Finlayson in the background.

Up to the mid-1950s, though, travellers entered Victoria by a different route. Later known as Highway 1A, this route can still be

Jack Most

Jack Most

Another endangered species, Garbage Gobblers were hatched in Langford.

traced by leaving the present No. 1 near Langford Lake on Gold-stream Avenue and following it through the suburb of Langford.

Along this route can be found an almost forgotten relic of the past. In the little Veterans' Memorial Park on the southeast corner of Goldstream Avenue and Veterans' Memorial Parkway (near the corner of the park farthest from the intersection) stands a refurbished Garbage Gobbler. It is appropriate that this bug-eyed, owlish creature (one of the last of his kind) should find a home in Langford because it was here that these distinctive garbage cans were manufactured. Designed by Len Shaw for the British Columbia Parks Branch in the late 1950s, the early concrete images (of which this is one) were later succeeded by fiberglass models that could be spotted around the province through the 1960s and 1970s. They expressed a developing concern of the time that litter should not be casually tossed out the window of a moving car. (Other provinces had similar schemes. In Manitoba, spherical receptacles meant to look like satellites invited travellers to "put your trash in orbit". Strangers to the province might have wondered apprehensively what was about to happen to them when a roadside marker announced, "Orbit in 10 seconds.")

Travellers who stop to pay their respects to the Garbage Gobbler can continue along Goldstream Avenue past the century-old Royal Colwood Golf Club until they come to a T-junction at the Island Highway (also known as the "Old" Island Highway). Traffic that turns left here will describe a long arc round the upper reaches of Esquimalt Harbour, passing through the old suburban town of View Royal and nearly touching the modern highway as the older road rounds the top of the inlet. From this point, one option is to make for downtown Victoria by way of Craigflower Road through Esquimalt, entering the city centre by way of the Johnston Street Bridge. Called the "Blue Bridge" because of the colour of its superstructure, this bascule bridge had a span that opened by means of a counterweight. Built in 1924, it carried vehicles on a wooden deck until 1966 when it gave way to steel grid decking. Construction on the bridge's replacement began in 2013.

The main route of the old highway, however, crossed the channel known as the Gorge at Admiral's Road. Craigflower Bridge, which crosses the Gorge at this point, was another venerable structure that came up for replacement in 2013. The old bridge had carried vehicles across the Gorge for nearly 80 years.

Long before an old alignment of the TCH passed close to its shores in the heart of Victoria, the Gorge Waterway inspired this lovely 19th-century watercolour.

E. Sandys / National Archives of Canada / C-024165

On the far side of the bridge, the old route followed the Gorge Road for about five kilometres—passing a series of motels—until it joined what became the modern route at Douglas Street. In fact, it was not—and is not—just two streets coming together at this major intersection. Although the confluence of Gorge Road, Douglas Street, Hillside Avenue and Government Street is controlled by traffic lights today, from the late 1940s until 1963, this was the site of Victoria's famous—or infamous—roundabout. Traffic circles have gone in and out of fashion since those days (and are "in" again, one should add), but this strange intersection—complete with a large circular lawn and a fountain dating from the days when horses were watered here—was a hub that left many visiting motorists feeling confused and bewildered.

Today, it is not too difficult for a navigator to find Douglas Street running south from this point through the city centre. This is—as it has long been—the final leg of the Trans-Canada Highway. The approach to downtown brings motorists past Paul's Restaurant at the corner of Douglas and Chatham. Paul's has been serving up home cooking since the mid-1950s. As they walk in, patrons are greeted by a collage of black-and-white photos from the establishment's early days.

Clark Saunders

Paul's Motor Inn and Restaurant in Victoria dates from the 1950s.

Though some things on the last few kilometres of the highway's route have changed over the years, much of Victoria's downtown remains recognizable. Near the harbour, Douglas Street passes the back of the landmark Empress Hotel. Having tea at the Empress—a tradition dating back more than a century—is perhaps the custom that best sums up the tourist's impression of a city that has for many decades done its best to out-English the English. In 1965, the hotel seemed so dowdy and old-fashioned that there were questions about its survival. Today, it shows unmistakable signs of life under Fairmont management.

Many of the Empress's neighbours survive from the late 19th and early 20th centuries, although sometimes with a changed purpose. After Canadian Pacific ferries stopped calling here in 1960, the former terminal building spent some years occupied by a wax museum before becoming home to the Robert Bateman Centre, housing a collection of the painter's work. At the opposite corner of the harbor, the iconic art deco tower of the former Imperial Oil Service Station (built in 1930, closed in 1974) has for many years now signaled the location

Peter St. John

Those who suggested-closing Victoria's faded Empress Hotel in the 1960s were overruled by a plan to breathe new life into the city landmark.

Brian Wolitski / bmwphotos.smugmug.com

Above: Across most of Western Canada, great blue herons can be seen standing, statue-like, in wetlands. But in Victoria, these elegant birds can often be seen perched, usually one-legged, in the upper limbs of a huge redcedar in Beacon Hill Park.

Below: Beacon Hill Park has been welcoming visitors since 1882.

Jack Most

of the Visitors' Information Centre. On Douglas Street itself, the old Crystal Garden with its swimming pool, art gallery and arboretum has been incorporated in an expanded convention centre. The provincial legislative building looks as it has throughout its history, right down to the strings of lights, lending a fairy-tale quality to the serious business of government. And just to the west of the building, the Tally-Ho horses continue to ply their trade as they have for well more than a century. However, the wagons with benches that could accommodate numbers equivalent to a small bus tour are no longer in evidence, having been replaced by elegant white carriages designed to carry more intimate parties.

On the opposite side of the legislature, the excellent Royal British Columbia Museum's present home did not appear until 1968, but in neighbouring Thunderbird Park, Mungo Martin House, built by the First Nations chief and highly regarded totem pole carver, dates from 1953. Examples of Martin's work can be seen here and in Beacon Hill Park where the totem pole that faces the ocean on a spot sacred to First Nations people was the tallest in the world when it was erected in 1956.

It is along the west side of the park that the TCH (still Douglas Street here) runs on its last kilometre. Beacon Hill Park, with its Douglas fir, arbutus, redcedar and Garry oak

Jack Most / themostinphotograpy.com

trees—all distinctive of the West Coast—has been providing respite for residents and visitors alike for more than a hundred years. The park includes features that have appeared in recent decades—the putting green and the petting zoo, for example—but midcentury tourists would have enjoyed its gardens as well as the pebble bridge constructed in 1945 in memory of the artist, Emily Carr—a gift from her sister.

The Trans-Canada Highway ends (or begins) at "Mile 0" where Douglas Street intersects with the shoreline's Dallas Road. A sign has marked the spot since the Victoria Automobile Club put one up in 1958. Its much-photographed current successor is a wood-and-stone affair that is maintained by the British Columbia Automobile Association.

Terry Fox—who is memorialized in a statue near this spot—was born in the year the Mile 0 sign was first erected. He was a baby boomer who began life in Winnipeg and as a young boy moved with his family to the West Coast. Later, with his Marathon of Hope, he set out to cross the country the hard way. Though he didn't make it (his heroic run ended near Thunder Bay, Ontario), the statue captures his vision as it suggests a different outcome. Placed here in 2006, it depicts Terry running toward the beach with his face set toward the Strait of Juan de Fuca and the towering Olympic Mountains on the farther shore.

The Mile 0 sign in Victoria is not the first to stand on this spot, while the Terry Fox statue is a 21st-century addition to the TCH's western terminus.

Jack Most

"Dreams are made possible if you try"

"Somewhere the hurting must stop..."

TERRY FOX
1958 - 1981

GO WEST, YOUNG MAN
(but first, GO SOUTH)

Getting to "The Coast" in the two decades after the Second World War was not an easy matter. In 1945, most Canadian roads were unpaved, and although 20 years later it was possible to cross Western Canada on pavement, routes south of the border consistently offered better options for those who were prepared to go out of their way. Where Canada offered gravel, the United States provided hardtop. When, in the late 1950s and early '60s, Canada was able to provide two lanes on major routes, the U.S. had moved on to develop four-lane interstate highways.

Some Canadian motorists tended to stay on the northern side of the border except for those stretches where to do so they would have had to travel on gravel. Others would head for the U.S. as soon as they could and not turn northward again until they were near their destination. Manitobans, for example, would drive south from Winnipeg on Highway 75 or from Brandon on Highway 10. Some then travelled west on U.S. No. 10 (later replaced by Interstate 94) through Fargo and Bismarck, North Dakota. Others, dipping not quite so far into the States, would take the No. 2, which runs through Grand Forks, Rugby (which claims to be the geographical centre of North America) and Minot. In the northwest corner of the state this highway passes through Williston where, through most of the 20th century, oil lay underground, untapped and waiting for its moment to transform the local economy and the surrounding landscape.

However, many travellers found that the No. 2, as it proceeds through northern Montana, was as dull as the proverbial ditchwater. The name of the town called Havre might have suggested something exotic, but its local pronunciation (*Haev*-er) quickly dispelled any such illusions. Even the knowledge that the town of Shelby had won passing fame as the site of a world heavyweight

Opposite: Montana's Glacier National Park places a significant focus on history and "parkitecture", including the spectacular Going-to-the-Sun Road. Completed in 1938, the highway is always popular and on long weekends, traffic moves at a walking pace, perfect for enjoying the spectacular views.

Opposite: Mountain Walrus / www.en.wikipedia.org

Peter St. John

Travel Manitoba

Above: Pompey's Pillar, named for Lewis and Clark's expedition guide Sacagawea's infant son, who was nicknamed "Pompey." The easily seen outcropping still bears William Clark's signature.

boxing match between Jack Dempsey and the long-forgotten Tommy Gibbons in 1923 could hardly relieve the tedium.

Consequently, many who started out on the more northerly route dropped down (via Williston, North Dakota and Glendive, Montana) to the No. 10 as they set out on the longest stretch of the journey across the state that became known as Big Sky Country. From the farm and ranch land of the east to the mountain ranges of the west, Montana was a state that took a long time to cross. Much of it was cowboy country. Towns like Miles City were known for the large steaks they served in their restaurants and for the impressively long bars at which a cowboy boot might rest on a rail. For breakfast, this was the state in which to order hotcakes—or the even more filling buckwheat cakes. Whatever currency you used to pay for your grub, the change was likely to include silver dollars. In Montana, folks would declare their independence by eschewing paper currency where possible and by declining to post a speed limit on the highway.

This was also Lewis and Clark country. In 1806, the expedition stopped by the large rock formation now known as Pompey's Pillar, located northeast of Billings. Clark left his mark on the pillar—literally—and his signature can still be seen today.

The highway still passes near the site, with its large interpretive centre (or center, as it would be spelled in the U.S.), before going on to the three "B"s: Billings, Bozeman and Butte. It is at Billings that I-90 joins I-94. It is I-90 that gives its number to the modern route (formerly the No. 10 Highway) that proceeds from Billings westward.

We are in mining country now. Beyond Butte and near the Great Divide, the town of Anaconda is still easy to locate by means of its old smokestack. The tallest masonry structure in the world, the smelter stack was in operation when midcentury travellers watched for the landmark. The smelter itself has since closed, but the monumental smokestack stands its ground.

Banjodog / www.en.wikipedia.org

Anaconda's smokestack has given up smoking.

Missoula is the most westerly of Montana's small cities. Located in forest country, its beauty was not always easy to see in the 1950s and '60s when pulp mills pumped pollution into the atmosphere.

As it crosses the narrow northern neck (known as the Panhandle) of Idaho, the Interstate negotiates its way past the town of Wallace on a viaduct constructed in 1991. Prior to that, the route went through the mining town on a street that was formerly designated as Highway 10. Until the viaduct was built, the locals could boast that an intersection in town was marked by the last traffic light on I-90—a route that extended from Boston to Seattle.

In northern Idaho, mining towns like Wallace and Kellogg have declined in population in recent decades; in any case, they were rather shabby places in their heyday. Coeur d'Alene, on the other hand, has always benefitted from its attractive setting on the lake of the same name. In fact, in the last half century, a burgeoning tourist industry has contributed to traffic congestion that can slow transcontinental traffic is it threads its way through the neighbourhood.

Peter St. John

Drivers past and present who stuck to the more northerly No. 2 Highway will have found that the dullness of the route suddenly gave way to spectacular scenery in the area of Glacier National Park. Those who did not take advantage of earlier opportunities to drop down to the No. 10 (now I-90) would link up with it at eastern Washington's metropolis, Spokane.

A prairie dog lookout. Once remarkably abundant across the Great Plains, the little rodents were on the verge of extinction in the mid-20th century. Thanks to protection programs in the Dakotas, they are again on the increase.

The second largest city in the state, Spokane began and ended the 20th century with several decades of slow growth. Travellers who caught it in the early postwar years, however, found it in the midst of a growth spurt. Bing Crosby had long since left his hometown by the time the Second World War came to an end, and a new century would arrive before the old Clemmer Theater would be renamed in his honour.

Until the completion of the beautiful North Cascades Highway (No. 20) in 1972, the most northerly route to the coast from Spokane

Steven Pavlov / www.en.wikipedia.org

Dry Falls. What must it have looked like when it was wet?

was the No. 2. The route passed close to the Grand Coulee Dam on the Columbia River (begun in 1936). No less impressive are the neighbouring Dry Falls, a five-kilometre long scalloped precipice, all that remains of what was likely once the largest waterfall in the world. Estimated at between five and 10 times the size of Niagara, to see it in operation you would have had to show up near the end of the last glaciation, when mighty waters repeatedly flooded this part of the country.

Highway 97 coming down from the north joins the No. 2 west of Dry Falls. They run southward together to Wenatchee. Having doubled in size since the mid-20th century, this is the largest community between Spokane and the coast. The route continues northwestward until, shortly before Leavenworth, Highway 97 splits off again and leaves No. 2 to continue on this trajectory on its own. Leavenworth was a struggling resource town until 1962 when it decided to draw in the tourists by reinventing itself as a faux-Bavarian village.

The impressive Cascade Mountains were bound to draw more visitors as winter sports became more fashionable in the later decades of the 20th century. Today, the area around Steven's Pass abounds in attractions for skiing enthusiasts. On the far side of the pass the highway follows the rushing Skykomish River down toward the Pacific. Of the places along the way, Monroe is the community that has been most dramatically transformed over the past half century. In the 1990s, the sleepy little place suddenly felt the effect of its proximity to the north-south I-5 corridor and mushroomed in size.

It is at the city of Everett that the No. 2 Highway links up with the I-5 (formerly Highway 99). This is the point at which trans-continental Canadian travellers would turn their vehicles northward and head for the border. (Those whose destination was Victoria might drive west from Mt. Vernon to the costal town of Anacortes, Washington, and take the ferry to Sidney on Vancouver Island. The ferry route is still in business, run today as part of the Washington State system.) The mainland route passes through the city of Bellingham, still a popular destination with cross-border Canadian shoppers.

Since 1921, the border crossing at Blaine has been marked by a Peace Arch. Built by Sam Hill, an American who was a leading figure in the good roads movement in the Pacific Northwest, it is one of the several structures in the region created out of Hill's favorite building material, concrete. Folks passing through the area in 1952 had a chance to hear the great African-American bass, Paul Robeson, performing at the border. The Red Scare of the McCarthy era was responsible for the left-leaning Robeson's being prevented from travelling out of his native country. The only way he could sing to a Canadian audience was to perform from the flatbed of a truck set up on the American side of the 49th parallel.

Beyond the border, the designation "99" still applied to the highway that continued northward to New Westminster and Vancouver. Named the King George Highway in honour of George VI, the route merged with the TCH in Surrey before depositing travellers in Canada's West Coast metropolis.

The High Fin Sperm Whale / www.en.wikipedia.org

The Peace Arch at the Canada-U.S. border crossing at Blaine, Washington.

the NUMBER 3 HIGHWAY
— THE CROWSNEST ROUTE

I t was 1962 before motorists who wanted to travel entirely in Canada could count on driving on hard-surfaced roads all the way from Manitoba to the West Coast. Until then, those who wanted to avoid as much as possible crossing the border into the United States tended to opt for the No. 3 Highway for at least a portion of their journey. Also called the Crowsnest route, after the mountain pass that took it through the Rockies, the more southerly No. 3 splits from No. 1 at Medicine Hat, Alberta, and is reunited with it at Hope, B.C. Until the early 1950s, even people driving from Medicine Hat to Calgary often avoided No. 1 and opted instead to take No. 3 as far as Fort Macleod before driving north on No. 2 to the Stampede city. The route was longer than No. 1 (although the TCH followed a longer path then than it does now, so the difference was not as great as it has since become) but No. 2 and 3 were almost entirely paved, which No. 1 was not.

Even tourists who wanted to include Banff in their travels might stay on No. 1 only until they got to Eisenhower Junction. Ahead of them—until the late 1950s—lay a mixture of paved and unpaved sections between Lake Louise and Golden. And beyond that, until the Rogers Pass section of the TCH was opened in 1962, lay the interminable stretches of unpaved road called the Big Bend. It seemed better to many to head south on Highway 97, picking up No. 3 near Cranbrook before continuing west. But until the late 1950s, it was not possible to drive from Cranbrook to Vancouver without either putting up with several dusty kilometres of gravel between Rossland and Christina Lake or taking a long detour south to Kettle Falls, Washington, and back up again to Canada.

Clark Saunders

Above: St. Eugene Mission Church near Cranbrook, B.C.

Opposite: Crowsnest Lake with Crowsnest Mountain in the background.

Opposite: Jerry Kautz

Wheateater / www.en.wikipedia.org

The southern Alberta landscape through which Highway No. 3 runs includes the Milk River Valley, with its fantastic stone formations and fascinating pictographs. It has been compared to stumbling upon a cathedral in the desert.

The sensation is particularly dramatic when viewed from the northern valley rim, looking across to Montana's smoky Sweetgrass Hills in the distance.

For those who, in the middle of the last century, opted for No. 3 all the way, the road beyond Medicine Hat followed a path through southern Alberta that was not much different from the four-lane route of today. Then, as now, it passed through ranchland. This is the part of the country to which Mormons came when they migrated north from the United States. Seven Persons, the first town encountered on the route, is also the first town with a historic Mormon presence. After running southwest as far as Seven Persons, No. 3 bends westward, keeping the Oldman River on its right for most of the highway's journey through southern Alberta. Irrigation was introduced to the Bow Island district in 1950. At Taber, it was making a difference as far back as the 1930s. There it helped the area to produce sugar beets and to become famous for its corn. The ethnic mix in this part of the country has included Japanese Canadians who were forcibly resettled here during the Second World War.

Coaldale's proximity to Lethbridge (Alberta's fourth largest city) has contributed to the town's significant growth since the middle of the last century. A much grander highway now than it was half a century ago, No. 3 still runs right through the middle of Lethbridge, arcing slightly to the south, then slightly to the north before exiting across the Oldman River. Much has changed in the city since the mid-20th century. From a population of 30,000 in 1957, it has grown to nearly 90,000. But some old landmarks—like the viaduct known as the High Level Bridge, built in 1909—re-

Galt Hospital, Lethbridge, Alta.

Courtesy of The Galt Museum and Archives / www.galtmuseum.com

main. And the landscape with its coulees—so typical of southern Alberta—communicate a sense of wild remoteness.

The growth of Fort Macleod has been much less dramatic than that of its much larger neighbour to the east. But in the early post-war years, this historic town was already offering much to attract the interest of travelling families. The old NWMP fort was providing entertainment with its musical ride. The vintage Empress Theatre (1912), which has become a home to live entertainment, was still showing movies. Today the highway still runs right through town, although it is now split between two one-way streets: 25th Street for westbound traffic, 23rd Street for eastbound. The streets still run past some vintage motels that contribute to the sense you can get at Fort Macleod of having stepped back in time.

West of the ranching country around Pincher Creek, the highway follows one of the few significant realignments to have been introduced since 1965. Today the road makes for Lundbrek by means of a virtually straight diagonal line through Cowley. In 1965 it was still doing a west, then north, then west jog reminiscent of the old No. 1 in western Manitoba.

Long before they reach this part of the country, motorists have seen the Rockies looming on the horizon. Today, the communities on the Alberta side of the Crowsnest Pass (at 1,358 metres, the lowest elevation of any pass through the Rockies south of the Yellowhead) are part of a single municipality that has reinvented itself as a tourist destination. But in the 1950s, Bellevue, Blairmore, Coleman and

Built in Lethbridge in 1910, Galt Hospital served as a medical centre and nursing school until 1955 when, likely in response to Canada's postwar polio epidemic, it became a rehabilitation centre until 1965. Then, renamed the Alexander Galt Museum (and, more recently, the Galt Museum and Archives) its expanded premises host exhibits of many kinds.

Frank were shabby little towns that had not emerged from their coalmining past and the dangers and economic uncertainties that went with it. Although the site of the Frank Slide would not acquire a visitors' centre for many more years, motorists driving through the field of boulders that were left when a huge chunk of Turtle Mountain broke away in 1903 could not help but feel awestruck. Efforts to have the spot designated a national historic site in 1958 failed. It was only in 1985 that the interpretive centre was opened.

In the 1950s, the communities on the British Columbia side of the pass were, if anything, dingier than their neighbours in Alberta. Michel and Natal were dirty and grimy, their unpainted buildings covered with coal dust. In 1964, the B.C. government, concerned about the ugliness and potential environmental impact of these economically depressed communities, relocated the residents to the larger town of Sparwood.

With its economy thriving today on the dollars spent by alpine sports enthusiasts, it is hard to believe that Fernie was once just another mining town trying to survive in the boom-and-bust cycles of the mining industry. It is no longer just a place that people pass through; it has become a destination.

By the time it reaches Fernie, the Crowsnest route has already begun its long winding way through British Columbia, travelling

More than a century after the entire east face of Turtle Mountain came thundering down, spewing limestone boulders bigger than houses across the valley floor (and burying the town of Frank), the disaster still looks unsettlingly fresh.

Peter St. John

great distances north and great distances south to get around ranges of mountains. At Cranbrook, the largest centre in the East Kootenay region, the highway strip has grown considerably over the years and the town centre has been spiffied up. From here the highway turns southward, crossing and re-crossing the Moyie River and passing the shores of Moyie Lake. At Creston travellers

Henry James Warre / National Archives of Canada / C-058135

were—and still are—surprised to see grain elevators so far from the prairies. In the early 1960s, a new section of No. 3 was built, climbing westward over the mountains from Creston to connect with the No. 6 Highway at a spot south of Salmo. Until then traffic was routed north from Creston on what has since become the Number 3A. This long and winding road still hugs the shores of Kootenay Lake. Half way between Creston and the ferry that takes them across the lake, motorists can still spot the Glass House. Beginning in 1952, a mortician named David Brown constructed the house out of 61,000 square six-ounce formaldehyde bottles.

Motorists passing through the bountiful marshes of the Creston Valley in the mid-20th century would have viewed a scene much like this one, painted in the mid-19th century.

The ferry that crosses the lake today is the successor of past generations of vessels that have transported vehicles to the western side of Kootenay Lake and the stretch of highway that still leads on to Nelson. In recent years Nelson has reclaimed and restored its impressive stock of vintage buildings. From here the old highway (now 3A) led on to Castlegar, a much less significant town in this part of the province in the 1950s than it has since become. The lead and zinc mining town of Trail has had its place on both the old and new No. 3 highways, but its neighbour, Rossland, has been sidelined since the modern highway was built from Kinnaird to Christina Lake in the early 1960s. (Gold mining was Rossland's industry in the past. The skiing industry keeps it going today.) The new road replaced a more southerly dusty gravel trail that had been carved out in 1922. Connecting Rossland with Cascade, this road was so uninviting that many motorists chose to make a long detour down through the U.S.—44 miles down to Kettle Falls and 36 miles back up to the border again; 80 miles of pavement to avoid about 20 miles of gravel.

West of Christina Lake the road that leads to Grand Forks has changed little over the years. At this point travellers are in the middle of Doukhobor country. The area has now embraced the role that this Russian Christian sect has played in local history (there is a museum devoted to their story at Castlegar, and you will even find borscht on some restaurant menus in the area), but in the years after the Second World War members of the group—largely because of the violence and arson associated with its radical Sons of Freedom

Peter St. John

With just 28 centimetres (or 11 inches) of precipitation annually, the disappearing shrub-steppe eco-system of the South Okanagan is Canada's only true desert.

Big sagebrush, ponderosa pines and bighorn sheep still greet those travelling through this "pocket desert".

branch—aroused suspicion and hostility from their neighbours and from the provincial government. The ruins of abandoned communal farm buildings can still be seen dotting the countryside.

At Grand Forks itself, Johnny's Motel by the river (just before the highway crosses an old truss bridge to enter the town) is still in business. Recently renovated under the ownership of a new family, it offered the novelty of an outdoor swimming pool as far back as the 1950s.

The "forks" which give the town its name are those of the Granby and Kettle rivers. From this confluence the highway keeps company with the Kettle and its valley for some distance westward.

On the next stretch of highway the road still passes through Greenwood, a one-time mining town with a checkered past. A brief boom more than a hundred years ago led to a bust when copper prices dropped after the First World War. During the next war it was one of those interior towns to which Japanese Canadians were forcibly moved. Some stayed on into the postwar decades, giving a distinctive character to the place.

The curiously named Anarchist Mountain commemorates a local radical of the late 19th century. Approached from the east it makes a relatively modest impression, but on the western side the many switchbacks of the descent into the Okanagan Valley at Osoyoos have always afforded spectacular views.

Today, as in decades past, travellers of the No. 3 Highway often find Osoyoos the hottest spot on their journey. Through the years Okanagan summers with their blue lakes and blue skies have encouraged visitors to linger. Midcentury travellers would have seen orchards up and down the valley. What they would not have seen is the vineyards that, over the past half-century, have made this one of Canada's prime areas for wine production.

Until the mid-'60s, the onward route from Osoyoos was via Okanagan Falls, south of Penticton. But finally a shortcut was installed. The modern route comes out in the Similkameen Valley. Summer travellers have always found it hard to pass up the produce stands around Keremeos.

The town of Princeton marks the eastern end of the Hope-Princeton

Peter St. John

Highway. Opened in 1949, the sharp corners of the switchbacks on this tortuous route have been smoothed out somewhat over the years, but it still makes an impressive ascent to Allison Pass—and an equally impressive descent down the other side. Near the summit the site of a midcentury forest fire used to be marked by the construction of a gallows by the side of the road with an enormous cigarette hanging from its noose. In case anyone did not get the point an accompanying sign bore the legend, "The one who dropped it should also be hanged"—a reminder that capital punishment was still in force in Canada in those days. The midsection of the Hope-Princeton Highway runs through E. C. Manning Provincial Park. Named for one of B.C.'s chief foresters, Ernest Callaway Manning (not to be confused with Alberta premier, Ernest Charles Manning), the park was established shortly after his accidental death in 1941, at a time when there was no highway access to it.

Courtesy of B.C. Forest Service

The approach to the west end of the Hope-Princeton Highway is marked by the junction with Highway 5 (the Coquihalla) and by the site of the Hope Slide. On January 9, 1965, the highway was buried by a landslide larger in volume than the Frank Slide (though the loss of life was smaller, with just four motorists killed). The enormous scar on the mountain can be seen today.

At the town of Hope itself, the No. 3 Highway and the No. 1 reunite today as they have done since the two highways were built.

Above: Today, many of the orchards that once marched down the western slopes of the southern Okanagan's dry hills have been replaced by vineyards.

Below: The B.C. Forest Service once took took a harsher view of forest fire prevention than Smokey the Bear. Below the giant cigarette in E.C. Manning Provincial Park the text reads, "The one who dropped it should also be hanged."

the YELLOWHEAD ROUTE

Opposite: Peter St. John

Although motorists travelling from Manitoba or eastern Canada to Saskatoon, Edmonton, Jasper, Prince George or Prince Rupert might opt to take the Yellowhead Highway, it has never been a preferred route for those who are looking for a direct way to what today is known in British Columbia as "the south coast". The No. 5 highway connecting the Yellowhead west of Jasper with Kamloops was barely completed by 1960. In 1965 (the end of the period covered by this book) most of it was still unpaved. At that time even Edmontonians bound for Vancouver would begin their journey by driving south to Calgary and from there take the No. 1 west.

Stan Milosovic

Named for the Rocky Mountain pass through which it travels, the Yellowhead Highway was not officially opened with that designation until 1970 when it was accorded status as a route of the Trans-Canada Highway. Prior to that various sections of the road had gone by a variety of numbers over the years. Today, it is No. 16 throughout its length, but in the 1950s, Manitoba listed it as No. 4 while Saskatchewan called it the No. 14 east of Saskatoon; to the west of the city it was part of provincial highway No. 5.

In the early postwar years, drivers seeking a more northerly route than the No. 1 Highway would find themselves zigzagging across the Prairie Provinces on unpaved roads, much as they would have done if they had stuck to the TCH. In Manitoba in 1946, only the 37-kilometre stretch from Gladstone to Neepawa and a short section shared with the No. 10 near Minnedosa were hard-surfaced. Until the early 1950s, when the Yellowhead's starting point was established west of Portage la Prairie, the road began by heading straight north from Portage before turning west toward Macdonald. Then as

Above: As the sign above indicates, some consider Winnipeg's Portage Avenue to be not only part of Old No. 1 West, but also the beginning of the Yellowhead Highway.

Opposite: West of the Rockies, motorists follow the scenic North Thompson River, photographed here in 1963.

Brian Wolitski

now, the highway went through Neepawa. But until the late 1960s, it also went through Minnedosa. The elaborate arrangement of bypassing highways constructed around the town in that period may have had something to do with the fact that the premier of the day, Walter Weir, made his home in Minnedosa.

In Saskatchewan, the highway went through more towns in the middle decades of the 20th century than it does today. At Yorkton—the largest town on the route east of Saskatoon—traffic flowed (or rather stopped and started its way) through the centre of the town. The more northerly semi-bypass route came later.

Some who have travelled across the Prairie Provinces have felt that when they reached the tiny hamlet of Dafoe at the west end of the Quill Lakes they had reached the mid-point not only of their journey from Winnipeg to Edmonton but between Saskatchewan's eastern border with Manitoba and its western boundary with Alberta.

For more than three decades, Saskatoon has been larger than

Those travelling the Yellowhead in autumn will likely see migrating flocks of sandhill cranes, above. Below, Saskatoon's lovely riverside park.

Peter St. John

Regina. But in the early postwar decades it was smaller than the provincial capital. Late 20th century growth would prompt the construction of Circle Drive to spare motorists the necessity of driving through Saskatoon's centre, but the city quickly spread beyond the eastern section of the bypass.

Having crossed the South Saskatchewan River in Saskatoon, the highway crosses the North Saskatchewan on its way to the largest town on its route in western Saskatchewan—North Battleford. Here again a bypass has superseded the through-town route travelled by earlier generations. There is no easy way of avoiding Lloydminster, however. The highway still has numerous traffic lights to slow traffic as it makes its way through the heart of the town that straddles the boundary between Saskatchewan and Alberta. The road from here to Edmonton was paved in the early 1950s, but its travellers still passed through a number of little towns that are bypassed by the modern four-lane superhighway.

It is a curious fact that the main trans-Canada routes through both Calgary and Edmonton go right through these busy cities. Unlike the city street that carries the route through much of Calgary, however, the highway through Edmonton was turned into a freeway in the later decades of the 20th century.

By 1950, the highway was paved west as far as Lake Wabamun

Magnificent Pyramid Mountain, just outside Jasper township, soars skyward to 2,662 metres or more than 9,000 feet, drawing admirers to the limpid waters of Pyramid Lake at its feet.

Peter St. John

Peter St. John

Above: Majestic
Mount Robson,
snowcapped even
during the summer
months, drew few
motorists before the
roads at its feet were
paved. A pity really,
for at 3,954 metres
(or 12,972 feet), it is
considered the most
prominent mountain
in the North American
Rockies.

Opposite: Once in
B.C., the Yellowhead
follows the North
Thompson River,
shown here in
a photograph taken
in 1963.

(and past the point at which the Alaska Highway—built during the Second World War—began its unpaved route northwestward). Ten years later the pavement had reached Jasper, but beyond the town site westbound traffic faced a long journey on gravel. Even those who headed south to Lake Louise on the Icefields Parkway (Highway 93) would have to wait another year or two before being able to complete the journey on pavement.

The Yellowhead Pass itself leads rail and road traffic across the continental divide from Alberta to British Columbia and from Jasper National Park to Mount Robson Provincial Park. It has the lowest elevation of any transportation route through the Canadian Rockies.

However, just as the builders of the CPR chose the Kicking Horse Pass and left the more northerly route to its later rivals, the southern highway was completed and paved before the Yellowhead route was in any shape to offer competition. In 1965, the road that passed majestic Mount Robson was still unpaved. A few kilometres farther west, travellers bound for Prince George or Prince Rupert on Highway 16 faced long stretches of gravel, while those who turned south toward Kamloops on Highway 5 encountered a road that was closed in winter. For almost its entire length, this stretch of highway followed the North Thompson River, virtually from its source all the way to Kamloops where the road connected with Highway 1. Less than 150 kilometres of this route—at its southern end—was paved. Small wonder that this route tempted few Vancouver-bound motorists until the later decades of the 20th century.

Opposite: Peter St. John

ACKNOWLEDGMENTS

I owe a debt of gratitude to many people who provided help and resources as I researched this book and drafted its contents.

Assistance of various kinds came from the staff of libraries and archives in the western provinces. Provincial highway maps from the period were made available to me by the staffs of the provincial archives of Manitoba, Saskatchewan and British Columbia and of the archives of the Glenbow Museum in Calgary. Tim Ross, reference and map librarian of the University of British Columbia, went above and beyond what I might have expected in order to be helpful.

Many journalists, archivists, museum staff members and local historians as well as business owners along the route were generous with their time in tracking down information about their particular locales. Among others I would like to thank Lewis Stubbs (University of Manitoba Archives), Carl Buehler (Moosomin, Saskatchewan), Ken McCabe (*Indian Head-Wolseley News*), Ike and Pat Reimer (former owners of the Safari Inn, Swift Current), Jennifer Barrientos and Tanya Field (Esplanade Archives, Medicine Hat), Steve Malins (manager of the Banff Park Museum National Historic Site), Nick Richbell (Canadian Pacific Railway Archives), Neil Finlayson (Sicamous and District Museum and Historical Society), Rene Bell Bourget (Three Valley Lake Chateau Ltd.), Don Lott (collections officer, Fort Langley National Historic Site of Canada), Chuck Chamberlain (owner of the Tomahawk Barbeque, North Vancouver), Carol Howie (West Vancouver Archives), Kelly Carty (Tunnels of Moose Jaw) and the people at Saskatchewan's Fieldstone Campground. I am also grateful to Mark Richardson for permission to use images of the Todd Medal, to Elmer G. Wiens for his image of the Old Yale Wagon Road sign, and to Brian Wolitski and Jack Most for their contributions of many superb images.

James G. Menzies, phytopathologist with Agriculture and Agri-Food Canada helped me with facts relating to the research station at Indian Head and with the subject of the disappearance of grain elevators on the prairies.

Among those who shared personal memories of travelling the Trans-Canada Highway in the first two decades after the Second World War, I want to thank my brothers, Tom and Allan Saunders. Roy Christie and his family were able to recall the experience of staying at campsites during those years.

Lesley Sisler was generous in providing comment on earlier drafts.

I am especially indebted to the travelling companions who shared my explorations of the highway. It was Jim Miller's sharp eyes that spotted the boundary stone in the woods where Ontario and Manitoba meet. But as the summary on the next page indicates, Doug Whiteway and Warren McDougall were the friends who shared much of the journey with me. For all their help I am most grateful.

This was very much a collaborative enterprise and I am grateful to the talented people at Heartland Associates for guiding this project to completion: publishers Barbara Huck and Peter St. John for their dedicated attention and resourcefulness, designer Bergdís Sigurðardóttir for her inspired design, and Dawn Huck for her skillful renderings of the maps.

The road is constantly changing, of course, and an accurate description of it and the places along the way would require constant updating. Responsibility for any inaccuracies that are not due to such changes rests entirely with me.

SOURCES

TRAVELS

September 5, 2011
(with Doug Whiteway)
—Manitoba-Ontario
Boundary to Winnipeg

May 21, 2012
(with Doug Whiteway)
—Winnipeg-Griswold,
Manitoba

June 10, 2012
(with Jim Miller)
—area around Manitoba-
Ontario boundary

July 20–26, 2012
(with Warren McDougall)
—Winnipeg–Salmon
Arm, B.C.

December 3–5, 2012
—Winnipeg-Langley, B.C.

May 27–28, 2013
—Abbotsford-Chemainus,
B.C.

July 28, 2013
—Chemainus-Victoria, B.C.

August 27–29, 2013
(with Doug Whiteway)
—present Highway 1,
Winnipeg-Abbotsford, B.C.

BOOKS

Bannerman, Gary and Patricia. *The Ships of British Columbia: An Illustrated History of the British Columbia Ferry Corporation.* Surrey, B.C.: Hancock House Publishers, Ltd., 1985.

Berton, Pierre. *The Last Spike: The Great Railway 1881–1885.* Toronto/Montreal: McClelland and Stewart, 1971.

Coo, Bill. *Scenic Rail Guide to Western Canada.* Toronto: Greey de Pencier Books, 1982.

Francis, Daniel. *A Road for Canada: The Illustrated Story of the Trans-Canada Highway.* North Vancouver, B.C.: Stanton Atkins and Dosil Publishers, 2006.

Granatstein, J. L. *Canada 1957–1967: The Years of Uncertainty and Innovation.* Toronto: McClelland and Stewart, 1986.

Guillet, Edwin C. *The Story of Canadian Roads.* Toronto: University of Toronto Press, 1966.

Hayes, Derek. *British Columbia: A New Historical Atlas.* Vancouver: Douglas & McIntyre, 2012.

Howarth, William. (Photos by George F. Mobley) *Traveling the Trans-Canada from Newfoundland to British Columbia.* National Geographic Society, 1987.

Kluckner, Michael. *Vanishing British Columbia.* Vancouver: UBC Press, 2005.

MacEachern, Alan, "Goin' down the road—for the first time." *The Globe and Mail,* August 18, 2012: p. F7.

McCourt, Edward. *The Road Across Canada.* Toronto: Macmillan of Canada, 1965.

McNally, Larry. "*Roads, Streets, and Highways*" in Building Canada: A History of Public Works. Toronto: University of Toronto Press, 1988: pp. 30–58.

Morton, Desmond. *Wheels: The Car in Canada.* Toronto: Umbrella Press, 1998.

Owram, Doug. *Born at the Right Time: A History of the Baby Boom Generation.* Toronto: University of Toronto Press, 1996.

Rataushk, Wes. *Silver Highway: A Celebration of the Trans-Canada Highway.* Markham, Ontario: Fitzhenry & Whiteside Limited, 1988.

Richardson, Mark. *Canada's Road.* Toronto: Dundurn Press, 2013.

Snyder, Tom. *Route 66 Traveller's Guide and Roadside Companion.* New York: St. Martin's Griffin, 2000.

Toppings, Earle, ed. *Canada.* Toronto: The Ryerson Press, 1967.

Wallis, Michael. *Route 66: The Mother Road, 75th Anniversary Edition.* New York: St. Martin's Griffin, 1990, 2001.

FILM

The Longest Road. National Film Board of Canada, 2003.